INTELLECTUAL FOUNDATION OF FAITH

Intellectual Foundation of Faith

by HENRY NELSON WIEMAN

PHILOSOPHICAL LIBRARY

New York

© Copyright, 1961
by Philosophical Library, Inc.
15 East 40th Street, New York

Library of Congress Catalog Card No. 60-13665

Printed in the United States of America

CONTENTS

INTELLECTUAL FOUNDATION OF FAITH

CHAPTER ONE

FAITH ASKS A QUESTION

The question asked by faith concerns not some one special kind of good. Rather it asks about the good of human life as a whole. It is not about any one of the many interests pursued in human life. It is about the direction in which all of life should move. Faith asks: What can save man from his self-destructive propensities? What can bring into action the depth and wholeness of man's being? Faith asks: What can actualize most completely the constructive potentialities of human existence? What can bring this partially created being to the full maturity of his powers and values? What can carry human history and human society and the individual to these attainments?

Religious faith is the endeavor to find a way of life which can draw into its current all the resources of human existence, both conscious and unconscious, both psychological and physiological, both the institutions of society and the course of history. Since this is what it seeks, the question must be asked with the wholeness of one's being and not alone with the intellect, although the intellect with all its powers must be drawn into the inquiry. The question asked with this significance and in this way is the question asked by faith.

Faith, when properly understood, is not merely a belief. Neither is it, necessarily, an optimistic attitude in the sense of assuming at the start that the way of life will surely be found. Rather it is a commitment of one's total self to this inquiry to find the way of man's creative transformation toward the greater good. The individual in the wholeness of his being is involved. It is commitment to what is supremely important, not alone for himself but for all mankind.

What is supremely important is not any belief. What is supremely important is the actuality which the belief seeks to apprehend. No belief ever apprehends any actuality completely and perfectly, least of all the actuality of what is sought by faith. Therefore the commitment of liberal religion is not to a belief but to the actuality which a belief seeks to apprehend; not to a problem solved but to a problem in process of being solved; not to an answer given but to a question asked and an answer found more or less adequate to the question.

Thus the faith of liberal religion reaches beyond all available answers to the actuality operating in human life about which we need to know more than is now known. Such a faith is in a sense an absolute faith because it does not depend upon any fallible belief or answer. It is absolute because it is founded not on an answer but on a question of such sort that when any answer is found inadequate, another and better answer is sought. In this way it can never be disillusioned, can never fail; it can always spring anew from every defeat. As in science, every error discovered only opens the way for further inquiry. So it is also with the commitment of faith practiced in liberal religion. One may very well live and die with the answer he has found. But the man of liberal faith dies with the answer he has found, not because it is the end of the trail; he dies there to keep the trail open for others to travel on beyond the point which he has reached.

One who is committed to religious inquiry does not assume that the question asked by faith has been fully and finally answered anywhere in any tradition or in any person. No tradition and no person has the answer all-inclusive and absolute; but many persons and many traditions have contributed something to an answer being slowly learned through the ages. It is as though humanity were a small child slowly learning how to articulate the question and seek an answer. But the child has not yet learned how to talk and think about these matters with clarity and understanding. Civilized man is a very young child, if his immaturity is judged by the brevity of his years in comparison with the years during which other forms of life have existed on this planet. Like most children he is inclined to think that great problems have been solved before they are even so much as understood.

The distinction between the two ways of approaching the religious personalities and traditions of history is of first importance. In the one way we view them as authorities having the right answer, if only we can understand what they have to say. In the other way, we view them not as authorities and not as having the right answer necessarily. Rather we view them as individuals and peoples who have struggled earnestly and persistently with the ultimate issues of life and death. They have become involved at that depth where the question is asked with all its full significance. They asked in faith, in the sense in which we are here using the word "faith." Their profound involvement exposes the issues in depth. We should study reverently their lives and their teaching to understand the issues. Otherwise we cannot even so much as ask the question with its full significance. These great souls call to us to join with them in the struggle to find a better answer.

The answer is not a verbal statement. It is a way of life.

A way of life can be found only by struggling with the issues. Only by undergoing a transformation in the organization of one's own personality and in society can the answer be found. It is a mistake to think that some teaching or some ideal will solve the problem provided that we accept the truth of it and live by it.

The problem will not be understood until we see that the human being, no matter how satisfied he may be at the superficial levels, is frustrated and falls into conflict within himself. The frustration and conflict are due to potentialities which strive to break free of the constraints placed upon them. The power and drive of these potentialities issue in self-destructive neurosis or self-destructive action. On this account the religious problem is rightly called the problem of man's salvation.

Man cannot live as do the other animals. Yet he has not found any other way fitted to actualize his potentialities in full measure. When he tries to do so, his actions become disruptive. For this reason society is chiefly concerned in suppressing the individual and blocking the full release of all his powers. Man's peculiar endowment demands a way of life which can be progressively constructive. But so far, every attempt at progressive construction has led in the end to progressive destruction. This gives rise to the religious problem. It is to find a way of life fitted to the potentialities of human existence, to release them most fully with constructive power.

Some have given up in despair and insist that man can never find in time and space, society and history, a way of life fitted to his creative potentialities. He must look to some other realm, they say, and they point in various directions to this other realm. Some say it is beyond history, without explaining what they mean by that. Some say that man's salvation is to be found in "the power of being." Some say it is to be found in heaven beyond death. Some say it is in Nirvana.

It is here contended that this despair is a mark of immaturity. It fails to see that human life is very raw and new. Man is a very recently developed form of life and even more recently developed is the way of life called civilization. Scarcely a moment in the clock time has elapsed since civilization began. To give up the search so soon is surely foolish. These men of despair are like the men who said man can never learn to fly and ridiculed all attempts to do it. But man has learned to fly. Against this illustration it must be said that what faith seeks is not a new machine; it is a creative transformation of man and society, releasing suppressed potentialities.

The religions of the world are only the first beginnings in the striving to discover the direction and order of life fitted for human existence. They are the first toddling attempts. Man has not yet learned to walk. He stumbles and falls constantly. All toddlers are like that. Must we then assume that he can never learn to keep his balance? Man is the most immature of all the creatures of the earth. He is in transition from the subhuman to something which he has not yet become. He is not only a very recent arrival on this planet, he is a very strange arrival, so different from everything else on earth that he has not yet found out how to live. We compared him to a toddler. But a toddler has a mother. So let us change the figure of speech and compare him to a chick newly hatched without a mother hen or brooder to care for him and without innate instincts to guide him, such as other animals have. Under such conditions it is no wonder that he has not yet found out how to live in a way suited to the demands which develop in him. Unlike the chick he does not know enough to seek refuge when the shadow of the hawk is cast upon the earth. The great religions point to the shadow of the hawk. But have they found the final refuge? That is the question.

Man's peculiar endowment makes it impossible for him

to find satisfaction in any state of existence which he has ever been able to achieve. In consequence of this he is, so to speak, a stranger on the face of the earth. While the rest of nature and the other animals seem to be at home in the world as it is now ordered, man is not at home. Every organization of life which he sets up, or enters, becomes in time like a prison to him, so that he must strive to break free of it and in this striving to break free of it he breaks it down. Often in doing this he breaks himself or stands in the midst of a ruin where once there was a structure. In this sense it must be said that man does not belong to the world as he finds it. Always there is a part of him, whether suppressed beneath the level of consciousness or not, which is hostile to the order of existence in which he finds himself, because it is to him a prison.

All the great religions in one way or another agree that this is the condition of man. But now comes the inference derived from the condition which is here disputed. The inference is that man can never find a way of life suited to his nature within the bounds of space and time, society and history. Therefore, so the inference runs, man must seek elsewhere to find what satisfies him in the depth and wholeness of his being. Since he is an alien to this world he must belong to another one, or, if not to another world, then to eternity beyond time, to the infinite which transcends every finite form of existence.

Liberal religion insists that this claim of the great religions is mistaken. It is here agreed that man is alienated from every state of existence in which he finds himself and that he will always be, so long as civilization continues. But this human condition can be interpreted in two ways. The great religions, excepting the Chinese, have given one interpretation of it. The other interpretation is that man is so endowed that he can never satisfy the essential human demands in any final state, not in Atman nor in Nirvana nor in paradise nor in the infinite power of being nor beyond history in any sense, nor in the so-called awe and wonder and mystery of the cosmos. But he *can* find it in a continuous creativity which reconstructs every state of existence to expand his horizons continuously. This is a "beyond," to be sure, but it is not beyond space and time nor beyond society and history.

"Expanding horizons" is a poetic term and requires more precise specification. The term as here used means: (1) expanding the range of what one can know; (2) expanding the range of what one can control; (3) more important than either of the two just mentioned, expanding the range of what one can appreciate as good and distinguish as evil; (4) most important of all, expanding in depth and scope one's appreciative understanding of himself and of the unique individuality of other persons and peoples.

These four cannot be separated from one another without disaster. Destructive consequences ensue if knowledge and control are expanded without like expansion in depth and scope of values distinguished and persons and peoples appreciatively understood. Indeed expansion of knowledge and control in the long run depend upon the third and fourth dimensions just mentioned so that, if the former get too far ahead, they decline and fail. Expanding horizons, as the term is here used, means these four expansions moving more or less in unison.

Of the four areas of expansion the most important is the fourth because the others are created by it. One can expand the range of what he can know, control, appreciate as good and distinguish as evil only by learning from others, when "learning" means not only acquiring information but also undergoing reorganization of personality so that one internalizes the appreciations and discriminations of others, adding these to what he had previously acquired. This internalizing is not a mere reproduction. Rather one acquires the perspective of another person or people by integrating it into the perspective which distinguishes his own unique individuality.

When this integration does not occur, the acquisition from others disintegrates the personality or produces what has been called the "other directed" person. His own individuality is either suppressed or disintegrated unless preconscious processes integrate into his own unique individuality what he acquires from others.[1]

Here we have two interpretations of a fact upon which both parties are agreed. The fact is that man cannot satisfy the demands of his total being in any time and place, in any society or culture or age. The individual may suppress the urges and drives which are frustrated by the established structure of existence in which he lives his life; he may seem at the conscious level to be quite satisfied when these frustrations are suppressed. But psychological studies make plain that "discontent" (to use Freud's expression) is always there. In this sense man is always alienated, estranged, frustrated, imprisoned, discontented, walled in, because his total being, as developed in any civilization, always demands more than his world has to offer. This is the actual condition of man on which both parties to the dispute are agreed. The dispute arises when it comes to interpreting this condition.

The interpretation of liberal religion is that man is made for this world of time and space, society and history provided that he reconstructs it continuously, not alone by natural science and technology but also by reorganization of his own personality and society so that each individual can have a deeper appreciative understanding of other persons and peoples and can himself be appreciatively understood in greater depth, thereby expanding indefinitely the scope and depth of good appreciated and evils distinguished.

According to this understanding of the human condition man finds his salvation, his deepest satisfaction and the fullest actualization of his potentialities, in a creativity which operates in his own personality, in society and history, to reconstruct the world in such a way as to expand his horizons in the fourfold manner explained above.

This creativity is not omnipotent. It often fails against the inertia in man himself, in social institutions and in subhuman conditions. Indeed it never prevails unless man does two things. First he must give himself to it in ultimate commitment in the sense of repudiating so far as possible everything in himself which resists its demands. Second, he must search out and provide the conditions most favorable for the continuous and prevailing operation of this creativity in society, in history and in intimate personal relations. These conditions which must be provided are in part psychological, internal to the individual himself. They are in part institutional, requiring continuous modification of the social order. They are in part biological, requiring development of the sensitivities and other capacities of the biological organism of man. They are in part physical, requiring continuous reconstruction of the physical environment so that men can live together with maximum vitality, sensitivity and appreciative understanding of one another.

This creativity operates by way of interchange between individuals, peoples and cultures. This special kind of interchange is opposed by many other kinds which obstruct and suppress it. This special kind has two parts which must not be separated: (1) it creates appreciative understanding in depth between individuals and peoples; (2) it internalizes in each party the knowledge, skill and appreciations acquired from the others after these have been internally modified in the preconscious so that they develop the capacities of each person's own unique individuality.

This creativity is distinguished from everything else by one outstanding characteristic. It generates insights. These insights lead to deeper appreciative understanding of other persons and peoples; they lead to aesthetic perceptions more profound and vivid than previously possible; they lead to scientific generalizations more comprehensive, more precise and more coherent with other generalizations; they lead to greater mastery in the administration of social complexities; they lead to social organization releasing more individuals to actualize their potentialities in that relation to one another which is mutually sustaining and mutually stimulating.

One cannot gain a new insight by aiming to achieve it because one cannot know what it is until it has emerged in the mind. Before they emerge, insights are completely beyond the reach of the imagination. What is beyond the reach of imagination cannot be aimed at, specifically sought or intended. One may aim to have insights by providing conditions favorable for their emergence. But the insights which actually emerge cannot be intended nor sought because, prior to their emergence, they cannot be imagined. Furthermore, profound insights emerge by way of a reorganization of the personality of such sort that the individual, prior to this reorganization, is unable to accept, appreciate, understand or receive in any way the insight which finally comes. The insight which leads one to love persons previously hated, would have been violently rejected if the suggestion had come prior to the reorganization of the personality occurring with the new insight. The insight which leads one to accept an ideal more comprehensive of all possible good than any ideal previously accessible to imagination, would have been cast off as inferior if suggested to the individual before insight and reorganization of personality enabled him to apprehend the values in it. The same is true of other profound and new insights, whether they pertain to scientific theory, administration of social complexity or the organization of society providing for more freedom of individuals.

This inability to accept or recognize or seek the greater good until the proper insight and reorganization of personality has occurred, is an old sad story running throughout the length of human history. Also it appears in the life of every individual as he develops from infancy on to whatever limit this creativity may carry him. It carries some individuals far beyond the limits reached by others. This is not alone due to innate powers and limitations. More commonly, perhaps, it is due to absence of those conditions for some, and presence of those conditions for others, which must be present before creativity can carry the individual very far in that continuous reorganization of personality with emerging insights whereby his horizons expand.

What is true of the individual in this respect is true also of human society and human history. In some societies this creativity can bring forth insights and expanded horizons far beyond the limits reached in other societies. So also some periods of history can expand the range of what man can know, control, appreciate as good and distinguish as evil along with deeper appreciative understanding of unique individuality, doing this far beyond the limits of other periods. The tragedy of human existence is that these creative periods of history have seemed always to have reached a point where they become self-destructive. Perhaps Western culture has reached this point. This suggestion is only a surmise; it is not an assured statement. But the recognition of this possibility is of imperative importance because civilizations are likely to become self-destructive when individuals in positions of responsibility refuse to admit the possibility of it. Refusing to recognize the danger, they refused to undertake the task of providing those conditions under which creativity can continue to operate effectively in the lives of men belonging to that society. The voice declaring that common practices and cherished ways of life must be changed to avoid defeat and self destruction is always an unpopular voice. In a democratic society it is especially difficult to get a hearing for such a warning when the people take great pride in these cherished ways of life, setting them up as the basis on which to defend their feeling of superiority over a common enemy.

The Arabian Muslim defends his way of life in contrast to that of the Western Christian on the ground that it makes him superior to the pork-eating Christian who does not pray five times a day, does not accept the Truth about the law and the will of Allah and never even attempts to make a journey to Mecca. On the other hand, the Western Christian defends what he calls his freedoms. Among these freedoms is his freedom to lobby congress to serve special interests, his freedom to elect the most winsome and popular figure in disregard of competence, his freedom to reduce his religion to a medley of faiths incompatible with one another and unable to provide a unifying devotion which might provide maximum freedom for individuals in such relations that each would undergo creative development to a high degree.

The Western Christian takes pride in his way of life because it stands in contrast to communism, even as the Arabian Muslim takes pride in his because it sets him off in contrast to the Western Christian. The point is not that the Arabian way provides conditions most favorable for creativity, nor the Christian way nor the way of Communism. Rather the point is that the pride which each takes in contrasting his way to the other, blinds each to the basic problem. The basic problem is twofold. It is: (1) to search out and set up the conditions most favorable for creativity and (2) seek appreciative understanding of the opposing way of life in order to acquire from the "enemy" whatever virtues are there. Only in this way can creativity operate effectively in human life.

This analysis of the condition of man points to a major decision additional to the decision already mentioned. To understand the imperative nature of this decision let us briefly restate what has been said about the human condition.

Civilization develops certain insatiable demands which cannot be satisfied in any achieved state of existence. These demands reach out toward the infinite. Since these demands cannot be satisfied by any *achieved* state of existence, the sense of frustration drives men to struggle against the limitations imposed upon him. This struggle may be suppressed and do its damage within the psychosomatic organization of the individual, rather than breaking out in destructive action upon the social order or in action intended to impair the lives of others. It may manifest itself in irresponsible pleasure-seeking, using this device to keep out of mind one's responsibility for the difficult and complex problems of interpersonal relations and of society. This sense of frustration may manifest itself in many ways, all of which are destructive either of self or of others or of the social order or all three.

This is the problem of man. The major decision arises when we seek to answer the question: What should be done about it?

The choice which must be made can be stated thus: Shall we seek deliverance by way of an infinite, omnipotent and perfect Being or shall we seek it by way of a creativity in human life which is not infinite, omnipotent and perfect?

If we seek deliverance by way of the infinite, omnipotent and perfect, the decision involves an issue which has not been generally recognized until recent theological thinking exposed it. The exposure of the difficulty appears in the work of Paul Tillich, although many others go along with him and have reached the same conclusion independently of him. The issue may be stated thus: If we decide to seek our deliverance in the infinite, the omnipotent, the perfect, we can find these only in being itself or the power of being.

Not all the philosophers and theologians who reach this conclusion use this language, but the outcome is the same. Infinite, omnipotent and perfect are entirely inaccessible to any human understanding. They transcend every possible characterization whatsoever. Therefore, being itself or the power of being can give us no guidance, no direction, no form or order for the conduct of human living, *except by* religious symbols which are not descriptively true of the infinite. In that sense they are noncognitive.

In a later chapter the work of Paul Tillich will be examined systematically because of his present importance in the field of religious thinking. Here he is mentioned as one of the leaders making clear the issue involved. But the same conclusion is stated again and again in *The Handbook of Christian Theology* to which 71 living theologians have contributed.

This brings us to a clear view of the decision which must be made. If we seek our deliverance in something actually operative in human life in the form of creativity, which is accessible to the human mind, which has a direction and form of operation, which can be studied to discover the conditions required for its effective operation, then we do not seek our deliverance in a mystery entirely beyond the reach of all understanding. In such case we turn away from the infinite, the omnipotent, the perfect. Any operative reality in human life sufficiently understood by the human mind so that we can know the direction of its development and the conditions required for its effective operation will necessarily be limited, imperfect, not omnipotent. Tillich, along with the other theologians, and philosophers who go along with him, deny that the question asked by faith can be answered by anything operating in human life which man can understand in the way mentioned. They deny it precisely because they demand the infinite, omnipotent and perfect as providing the way of man's deliverance.

Here we have a major decision of utmost importance. Men have not ordinarily made the decision because the issues have been obscured. It had been thought that the infinite could be apprehended in such form as to guide and direct the course of life. But now it has been clearly shown that the infinite, omnipotent and perfect must necessarily be an impenetrable mystery. It is utterly inaccessible as a guide to human conduct, without form, structure or direction knowable to man. This has now been made known, the issue is clear and the decision must be made.

If one accepts as finally authoritative some one or more of the great religions, the decision has been made for him. He must seek deliverance by way of the unknowable, using non-cognitive symbols to give him the semblance of knowledge, and to strive without knowing what the infinite may require of him. If one does not accept as finally authoritative any one or more of the supreme religious personalities, he is free to decide between the impenetrable mystery on the one hand, and a knowable creativity on the other. But the decision must be made. We cannot straddle the two ways.

Of course there is mystery, no matter what we choose. No one is denying that. Complete and perfect and all-comprehensive knowledge man does not have of anything, not even of tables and chairs, much less of creativity. The question is not whether we can have complete and perfect knowledge. The question is whether we can have any knowledge at all, and whether we can have an increasing measure of knowledge, from devoted inquiry, so that we can act to provide the conditions under which the saving power of the divine presence can operate effectively to deliver man from his self destructive propensities by opening the way to expanding horizons. The term "divine presence" in this case refers not to the infinite, omnipotent and perfect, but to the creativity which generates insights expanding the horizon in four dimensions. If we decide for creativity, we must accept the fact that creativity is not omnipotent. It might fail. It may sometime come to an end. Whether it will or not, we do not know. Those who predict the inevitable decline or ending of all human life with its creativity, are just as naive as those who predict the inevitable continuation of human life forever onward and upward. The human mind is simply incapable of making such predictions. Least of all can it predict the future of creativity, because of its distinctive nature. Its distinctive nature is to generate unforeseeable insights expanding the range of what we can know, control, can imagine, can appreciate as good and distinguish as evil. Therefore any attempt to make final predictions concerning the destiny of human life endowed with creativity, is foolish and futile, whether the prediction be pessimistic or optimistic.

We have suggested two major decisions which faith must make in seeking the way of man's salvation. The first of these two, mentioned at the beginning of this chapter, requires us to decide whether or not to accept one or more of the supreme religious personalities of history as finally authoritative concerning the way of salvation. The other is to decide whether or not to seek salvation by way of the infinite, omnipotent and perfect or to seek it by way of creativity which is not infinite, omnipotent and perfect but which operates in human life under knowable conditions, many of which man can provide.

Let us now look at some of the insatiable demands developed in man by civilization, which make him self destructive when the way is not opened for expanding his horizons. One of these is the insatiable drive for vivified consciousness. Boredom is experienced when this drive is not satisfied. To attain vivified consciousness the individual seeks adventure, even danger and pain, and will accept suffering and destruction when vivified consciousness cannot be had in constructive action. Dostoievsky makes this very plain in his portrayal of human beings.

Another of these drives which make for discontent is a soaring imagination. The individual or the group strives to actualize some of these imaginary constructions, even at the cost of abandoning or destroying the established structure of things.

Another feature of human personality is the complexity of conscious and unconscious propensities and their conflict with one another. When this complexity with its inner conflicts cannot be organized for constructive action, it often drives to destruction of self and others, of social order and of civilization.

A fourth insatiable demand insistently develops in human life. Every individual experiences a crying hunger to be appreciated and understood in the depth and wholeness of his being. This appreciation and understanding he cannot find in the social relations accessible to him. In cases of rare good fortune loneliness may be assuaged but never entirely cured. Consequently he strikes out wildly to bring himself to the attention of other people, if not to win their affection, then at least to command their attention.

Another basic drive seeks freedom when freedom means to bring the wholeness of one's unique individuality into action instead of that mere fraction of the total self which conditions permit. The individual fights against the constraints which will not let him exercise the powers and resources of his own individuality.

These are the drives developing in human life. They cannot be satisfied within the limits of any established organization of the world and on that account demand a more or less continuous creative reorganization of the personality, of society and of physical conditions. They are the drive to vivify consciousness, the drive to carry into action the soaring imagination, the need to organize progressively the increasing complexity of the total person, the cry to be appreciated and understood in depth, and the drive for freedom beyond the limits of any social order.

Any or all of these drives can be suppressed in many individuals under certain social conditions. Perhaps under some conditions they can be prevented from developing very far, or anesthetized or even killed. There is always the danger that conditions will develop having this effect upon human beings generally, so that people move around more or less like automatons, occupied with trivialities and a mechanized routine. But always, sooner or later, some individuals break free of these inhibiting and deadening conditions. Such individuals become dangerous destroyers or creative leaders, depending on whether or not conditions frustrate intolerably or permit creative development.

This is the intractable make-up of the human being. The great artists portray it in literature and the other arts. Perhaps Freud has done most to open it to our awareness in psychology. The existentialists today are exposing it in philosophy and literature. But none of these have shown the way to solve the problem. The problem is to release the drives which will not be confined. This is the religious problem. Our hope is that faith may be induced to seek where alone salvation can be found. It can be found only in a creativity generating insights which release for constructive action the growing potentialities of human existence.

Especially we need to understand the difference between the moral problem and the religious problem if we are to deal effectively with man's misfit and find the answer to the question asked by faith. The moral question and the religious question are often confused. There can be no escape from self destruction if morality is not distinguished from religion. We must try to see both the distinction between them and the cooperative relation they can have.

The primary question which morality asks might be stated thus: What guiding principle distinguishes right moral conduct from wrong conduct? The problem of morality is to discover that course of action which will make the best possible out of human life within the limits of human vision. Vision here refers to the range of ideal possibility which the human mind can envisage at any given time, and man's understanding of the motivating currents of life by which the ideal possibility might be actualized.

The primary question asked by faith is different. It might be stated thus: What operates to expand the vision of man, so that he can do what he cannot now do to make life better? Man's power to improve himself and his world is limited by his vision, otherwise called his activating ideals, purposes and understanding of conditions. These cannot be rectified nor made more comprehensive by any vision man has at the time because it is precisely this vision which must be expanded and corrected. Therefore he must look to something which operates to transform him as he cannot transform himself by expanding the range of what he can appreciate as good and distinguish as evil. As suggested already, what does this is a kind of interchange between individuals and peoples creating in each the capacity to distinguish good and evil at depths and in forms not previously accessible. The religious problem is (1) to distinguish and disentangle this creativity from other kinds of interchange which obstruct and suppress it and (2) provide the conditions, psychological and social, under which this creativity can rise to dominance over counter processes.

Here we see the difference between morality and religion. Both seek to transform the life of man into the best it can ever become. Morality seeks to do it through human action directed by the best vision available. Religion seeks to do it by human action directed to providing the conditions under which a vision may be created more comprehensive and profound than any available at the time. Religious action providing these conditions may take the form of worship, meditation, self examination, repentance, acceptance of forgiveness and practices of commitment. These may serve to drive away the inhibitions and anxieties obstructing the emergence of insight. Song, ceremony and ritual may serve these ends. The practices of Zen Buddhism are an example of the most rigorous and extreme methods for providing the conditions under which a life-transforming insight may emerge. It is mentioned here to illustrate, not necessarily to adopt.

Moral action and religious action can do their work independently of one another. On the other hand, they can unite and merge into a single course of action, although the moral significance of that action will always be different from the religious significance. The moral significance will be the good achieved by action under the control of the vision of ideal possibilities already had. The religious significance will be action providing conditions favorable for the creation of vision yet to be attained. In this sense religion seeks a good beyond the power of man, meaning beyond the reach of vision had at any one time. In the language of worship, we pray for light and guidance.

A moral religion has responsibilities over and above the moral problem. These responsibilities pertain to the practices by which the individual and the group endeavor to bring themselves more completely under the control of the creativity generating insight and increasing the capacity to distinguish good and evil. Practices distinctively religious are intended to remove from the personality the dispositions, and from society the institutional conditions, which resist the creative transformation of emerging insights. These practices are called worship, ritual, prayer, religious assembly and ceremony, meditation, social action and other such exercises. Without these practices distinctively religious, it is impossible by deliberate intent to maintain, recover and improve the conditions, psychological and social, which are receptive to creative insight. The distinctive responsibility of religion over and above the moral problem is, therefore, to maintain and to improve these psychological and social conditions most receptive to "the voice of God," when the word "God" refers to what transforms man as he cannot transform himself, to save him from his self destructive propensities, and lead him to the best that human life can ever attain, provided that he meet the required conditions. It is here contended that the word "God," when it refers to what has the character and power to save man as he cannot save himself, must refer not to the infinite, omnipotent and perfect but to the creativity generating insights when these increase the range and depth of good appreciated and evil distinguished.

The primary purpose of worship is not to contemplate and adore a being of infinite glory, power and perfection, necessarily beyond all human knowing and therefore accessible only by way of non-cognitive constructions of the imagination, called religious symbols. Worship of this kind can give one an exalted feeling called religious experience. But it is a psychological luxury having little to do with the life and death struggles of the great personalities, whether in the Garden of Gethsemane or in the wilderness struggling with the devil for forty days and nights. The proper purpose of worship is to keep the religious problem at the top place in the conduct of man's life. Worship and other practices distinctively religious are vital and practical, determining the issues of good and evil. They are as necessary as food and drink. Food and drink are required for the body but creativity is necessary for everything distinctively human in the conduct of our lives. Religious practice rightly conducted is designed to keep ourselves receptive to this creativity, even as eating and drinking keep the organism receptive to the necessities of biological existence.

Religious practice rightly conducted must be concerned with "transcendence" according to the teaching of much theology. Many would say that we are not talking about religious faith at all if we do not consider the transcendent. Unfortunately, this word "transcendence" has many meanings. We cannot deal with the subject until we distinguish some of these diverse and contrary meanings and indicate which are essentially involved in religious faith and which are not.

Supernaturalists identify transcendence with supernatural-ism and would deny that any other meaning of the word is relevant. Many who reject supernaturalism still insist on transcendence, meaning infinity and mystery. Some phe-nomenologists and existentialists use the word to refer to the totality of immediate consciousness because this total fullness of awareness is not identical with, in that sense transcends, the world of objects known to science and common sense.[2] By "transcendence" Jaspers means the "encompassing." Still others mean ideals transcending actual existence. Various kinds of ontology specify different interpretations of what transcends all contingent existence. Therefore when one speaks of transcendence the hearer cannot know what is meant unless the meaning is specified; and often the speaker does not himself know what he means.

The divine creativity answering the question asked by faith is transcendent according to several meanings of this word. It transcends the human mind and the world known to science and common sense. It does so in this sense: It cre-ates the human mind and its world by way of creative inter-change. It does this for each individual, beginning with early infancy. The interchange develops between the infant or-ganism and what interacts with it, whereby the infant comes to understand and use the meanings of the signs and the language occurring around him. Until such signs and such language are understood and used there is no human mind in the infant and no world known to that mind.

Thus the divine creativity is transcendent because it is not the product of the human mind; rather the human mind and its world are the products of this creativity. In this sense it is ontologically prior to man's world and to man himself since every man and every man's world is created in this way. It creates them but is not separated from them.

In still another sense, this creativity transcends the human mind and the world known to common sense and to science.

To discern this second meaning of "transcendence" we look not at the new born infant undergoing creative transformation, but at the subhuman animal living many thousand years ago and undergoing transformation by creative interchange whereby it acquires a human mind and the kind of world which eventually became the world known to science and common sense in our time. Here again we see that the divine creativity transcends man and his world, not in the sense of being "outside of" it, but in the sense of creating it, sustaining it, developing it to larger dimensions and to higher dominance over the sub-human levels of existence.

In a third sense, the divine creativity transcends the human mind and its world. This third meaning becomes apparent when we note that the human mind in its present form, and the world as known to science and common sense today, are transitory and contingent, upheld by creative interchange and subject to radical transformation by this creativity. What this creativity will make out of the human mind and its world a thousand or ten thousand years from now we do not know, any more than primitive man with his mind and his world could foresee the mind and the world of Western man in the 20th century. What new heaven and earth, and what new mind of man, will be brought into existence by this creativity are entirely beyond the reach of human imagination. This is so because the different mind and different world will arise by transformation of man's imagination. Consequently, his present imagination cannot compass that other imagination yet to be created.

In a fourth sense, the divine creativity is transcendent. It creates in the awareness of immediate consciousness a fullness of concrete experience transcending all description by propositions. Art in its many forms, such as music, poetry, painting, dance and others, makes us more vividly aware of this rich abundance of immediate experience, defying description by propositions. In some forms of mystical experi-

ence this fullness of immediate experience floods consciousness so completely that it submerges all the forms and structures by which the world of common sense and science are
apprehended. Or if it does not entirely submerge, the mystical
experience gives to the world of common sense an abundance
of vivid qualities whereby it takes on glory and wonder beyond description. In still another kind of experience, this
submergence of structure beneath a flood of quality may
generate the experience of horror or "nausea," to use Sartre's
expression. Or the absence of structure may give the sense
of "nothing that nothings itself," or the sense of "absurdity."
These all are instances of transcendence when transcendence
means experience beyond the reach of those structures which
characterize the knowable world of practice, foresight, rational order and scientific theory.

This flooding abundance of sensed and felt quality is
relevant to the transcendence of divine creativity in this sense:
Creativity not only generates greater abundance of qualities
but also, when required conditions are present, creates by way
of innovating insights the structures giving to this abundance
of quality the forms of aesthetic depth and vividness. This
aesthetic depth and vividness of quality structured in this
way is called "love," "glory," "wonder," "beauty," "God," or
otherwise symbolized to express the highest attainment of
human life.

These four forms of transcendence characterizing the divine creativity should show that it is transcendent in every
sense in which "transcendence" applies to what creates, upholds, saves, and transforms toward the highest attainment of
human life. "Transcendence" has other meanings which do
not apply to the divine creativity, but these other meanings
are irrelevant, when not misleading, to a faith which seeks
the true answer to the religious question.

While every high endowment is brought to human life
by this creativity in the form of innovating insights, and while

this creativity is not the work of man but the work of God, man has his work to do and the duty to do it is imperative. Man should search out and provide the conditions, so far as he is able, under which this creativity can operate to bring forth the new insights. Also, after the insight has emerged, he must develop it, find out how to apply it, and bring the complex order of his existence into conformity with its demands. For example, after the insight has emerged that all human beings are participants in creative interchange and none should be deprived of participation to the limit of his ability, slavery and exploitation stand condemned. But the institutional structure of society and the established habits of life are not changed to meet the demands of this insight. This continuation of the old ways, resisting the demands of the new insight given to man by the divine creativity, magnifies the evils of slavery and exploitation. Or again, the insight arises that all nations and peoples must have that relation to one another and that level of well-being required for creative interchange, full and free between each and all, else misery and destruction will spread and grow. This is the "voice" of divine creativity speaking to man. But the old institutions of exclusive nationalism and racial antagonism still persist.

The divine creativity brings forth the transforming insight. This man cannot do. This is the transcendence of the "Word of God." But after the divine creativity has thus spoken in the form of an innovating insight, man's work and man's responsibility are to obey. The evils of human history are largely the result of man's refusal to develop, apply and carry through the demands of the "Word of God," when this expression is understood to mean not merely what is written in a book called the Christian Bible, but also the actual, operating and ever-present creative interchange between individuals and peoples, generating insights of appreciative understanding. The sin of the Christian tradition has been to reject this living "Word of God" by putting in its place a book written two thousand years ago. To be sure, the Bible can be used to promote this Living Word which speaks in creative interchange. But often it is used to exclude and deny this continuing creativity. When so used it becomes a great evil.

We have examined the meaning of "transcendence" as it applies to the divine creativity in creative interchange. We have found that this creativity is characterized by transcendence. It is transcendent in four dimensions. So we conclude: When faith seeks a transcendent answer to its question, that answer is given in the form of the divine creativity.

Civilization is the work of the divine creativity combined with man's refusal to obey its demands. As stated above, man's disobedience assumes two forms. He refuses to search out and provide the conditions under which creative interchange can operate most effectively; he also refuses to obey the insights created in this interchange when obedience requires that he reconstruct his institutions, his habits and his attitudes. The monstrous evils of civilization arise from this refusal to give first place above all else to the demands of creative interchange. On the other hand, the wisdom, nobility, knowledge, art, concern for individuality and other values arising with civilization are the work of the divine source of appreciative understanding and learning from one another. Thus civilization increases both the good and the evil of human life, the evil due to man's disobedience to the demands of creative interchange; the good due to man's acceptance of the insights arising out of this interchange and his action in obedience to them.

Nothing can be so nobly virtuous as the human level of existence reared to a peak by civilization; and nothing can be more cruel and destructive. But these two, the saintly and the demonic, are ambivalent. Both are ways in which suppressed human potentialities are released from the deadening constraint of social convention and institutions unfitted to release the potentialities of human personality. Saintly virtue has its darker side under such conditions, and demonic evil has a latent capacity for great good.

This character of civilization explains a strange fact about human history. The strange fact is that the great religions did not arise until two thousand years after civilization first began on the Nile, the Euphrates and the Indus rivers and, a little later, on the Yellow River. The world religions did not begin to develop until about 800 B.C. It is now possible to see the cause for this delay. Not until the human level of existence had been reared to a considerable height by two thousand years of civilization, could the question come clearly to consciousness which is asked by faith. Not until civilization had created the complexities, the inner conflicts, the suppressed potentialities and the wider dimensions of meaning carried by language and other symbols, could the religious problem of man be clearly discerned. So long as the development of the human level was confined within the iron bonds of the magic and tradition imposed in tribal life, the basic question asked by man about himself could not come forcibly to mind. So long as the insatiable drives are under the control of coercive tradition and tribal taboo, they cannot break free sufficiently to develop the power and intensity required to make themselves known with vivid insistence.

From about the time of the eighth century B.C. the increasing power of the confined potentialities in the human being gave rise to the great religions. There had always been religion. Tribal life had always been dominated and suffused by it. But it had been in great part a religion of taboos. Hence in tribal life religion does not so much release but rather serves to bind and restrain the development of unfulfilled potentialities. Religions arising after 800 B.C. strove to break free of these restraints. They reached after the infinite. Gautama Buddha, the great Hindu teachers, Laotzu, the Hebrew prophets, the Greek philosophers and tragedians, St. Paul and Zoroaster sought to cast off the limitations of the temporal world. They sought the infinite, the omnipotent and perfect to release the potentialities of the strange being called *homo sapiens*, because this creature finds the temporal world a prison and he storms for release. This was a good first approximation to the answer sought by faith. But it cannot be the final answer.

In our time civilization has built up the suppressed potentialities of man to a greater intensity than in the past. Consequently they demand release more insistently than ever. At the same time we know more about these suppressed potentialities. Also we are training men and establishing institutions devoted to the study of these suppressed potentialities and the problem of how to release them constructively. This is what every educational institution is supposed to be doing, whether or not it does it effectively. The National Institutes of Health in Bethesda, Maryland, financed by the government, are one among many institutions devoted to research into this problem. Also we have today vastly more power to reconstruct the order of human life, psychologically, institutionally, biologically, chemically, physically, than was ever possessed by man before.

These conditions are favorable for grappling anew with the religious problem. Perhaps we have come to a time when there will be a second break-through to a better answer than the past could reach, even as the thousand years after 800 B. C. was the first great step toward a solution of the problem. The literature of our time seems to indicate that many are more acutely conscious of the problem than men generally have been in the past few centuries. Psychological and social studies are proclaiming that the human endowment is a misfit in the world as now ordered. The existentialists, both theological and philosophical, are saying the same.

This social, psychological, historical situation gives to liberal religion its high vocation. As previously stated, liberal religion here means a faith asking a question and seeking an answer more adequate to the condition of man and human need than the answers most commonly proclaimed. Liberal religion stands in opposition to the faith which assumes that the problem of man has been solved and the final answer given. Liberal religion is the only form of faith able to take the next step by getting an answer fitted to the need of the magnified power, the magnified danger and the magnified constructive potentiality of our time. This it can do because it begins by asking a question. It does not begin, as other forms of faith have done, by proclaiming an answer before the question has been asked and an answer found fitted to the question.

In order to understand the question asked by faith, we have made certain distinctions. We have distinguished between faith and belief; between two ways to approach the religious personalities and traditions of history; between two ways to seek deliverance from self destruction; between the mystery of being and what truly operates to save and transform man as he cannot transform himself; between morality and religion; between the transcendence of creativity and man's responsibility; between the good of civilization and its evil; between religion which confines and religion which releases the constructive potentialities of human life.

With this understanding of the moral and religious problem of human life, it will be profitable to examine the work of some of the most influential men of our time who are working upon it. We shall look at John Dewey first, not because we think his explicit teaching has done more than any other to show the way, but he is more intimately a part of our American life than many of the others and we may find, underneath his explicit teaching, something of profound importance.

CHAPTER TWO

JOHN DEWEY ANSWERS

Only once did I meet John Dewey in person for a brief conversation between us two alone. There are meetings which we do not forget because of their significance. I should like to tell you about this one but I do not have the gift. Perhaps, however, I can suggest the impression Dewey made on me by setting it in contrast to a personal encounter had by another man which this other man describes in a rather striking manner. He was a poet who wrote a poem called "Roman Women." He was trying to suggest what he thought must have been the kind of women who helped to rear the power of ancient Rome. He does it by describing his meeting with an unknown modern Roman woman whom he passed as he walked through the city of Rome. His lines run like this:

> Close by the Mamertime
> Her eyes swooped into mine.
> Oh Jove supreme! What gleam of sovereignty
> What hate, large, disproportionate.

When I met John Dewey there were no swooping eyes and no gleams of sovereignty. I never met a man more simple, kind and gentle. Nothing striking about his appearance, rather very ordinary, so much so, that some philosophers who were opposed to his views went around saying that John Dewey was nothing but a New England farmer and no philosopher at all. For my part I cannot see how New England farmer implies absence of philosophic insight. But that is what they said about him not only because of his appearance and manner but also because he worked on problems of everyday life and not on those lofty themes which engage the minds of men who have swooping eyes and gleams of sovereignty.

I mention my only meeting with Dewey in person because I think it is an example of the kind of communication which Dewey believed to be more important than anything else in the world. I do not mean that this particular instance of communication which I had with Dewey is so important except for myself. Rather I mean that communication of a certain kind is what Dewey believed to be supremely important and the meeting I had with him was an example of this kind.

What a man believes to be supremely important is the living faith which activates his life. But the faith activating a man's life is not necessarily identical with the theory which he sets forth when he discusses the problems of religion. Indeed the contrast and opposition between his living faith and his theory about faith may give rise to ambiguities and confusions. I think that this is true of John Dewey.

A living faith runs deeper than words. It is often inarticulate. When such is the case, one must seek this living faith not in what a man says about religion. Rather he must find it showing forth in what the man says and does when he is not thinking about faith at all. When he begins to talk about religion he may become involved in arguments leading into issues which conceal his own personal religious commitment.

Dewey wrote a little book in the latter years of his life called *A Common Faith*. This book is supposed to set forth his ideas about religion. I shall discuss it later; but I am convinced that we do not find Dewey's own faith clearly articulated in that book. Rather, as I said before, you find his faith most manifest when he is talking about the important problems of human life which do not bear the labels of religion and where the word "faith" does not enter into the discussion.

I shall quote a passage where I believe Dewey indicates what is the most important thing in human life for him. The passage is found in his book *Experience and Nature*, pages 166, 205-6 and on page 490.

Of all affairs, communication is the most wonderful . . . that the fruit of communication should be participation, sharing, is a wonder by the side of which transubstantiation pales. When communication occurs, all natural events are subject to reconsideration and revision; they are re-adapted to meet the requirements of conversation, whether it be public discourse or that preliminary discourse termed thinking. Events turn into objects, things with a meaning. They may be referred to when they do not exist, and thus be operative among things distant in space and time . . . their meanings may be infinitely combined and rearranged in imagination and the outcome of this inner experimentation—which is thought—may issue forth in interaction . . . communication and its congenial objects are objects ultimately worthy of awe, admiration, and loyal appreciation. They are worthy as means because they are the only means that make life rich and varied in meanings. They are worthy as ends, because in such ends man is lifted from his immediate isolation and shares in a communion of meanings. . . . When the instru-

mental and final functions of communication live together in experience, there exists an intelligence which is
the method and reward of the common life, and a society
worthy to command affection, admiration and loyalty.
. . . Thus communication is not only a means to common
ends but is the sense of community, communion actualized.

Can we conclude from this quotation that the most important thing in human life for John Dewey is a kind of
communication? Whether or not this judgment is correct
about what Dewey esteemed most highly, we shall demonstrate that his discussion of ideals involves him in this position.
In any case, he fails to make clear the distinction between the
kind of communication supremely important and many other
kinds. Certainly he would not exalt to this high place in
human life the kind of propaganda reducing individuals to
puppets under the control of a dictator or an advertiser. And
there are many other kinds of communication, also, which I
am sure he would not glorify as he does the kind discussed
in the quotation.

The kind of communication supremely important for
John Dewey is the kind which creates community and communion between individuals and peoples. That much he
states explicitly in the quotation. It is the kind enabling each
to learn from others not only the knowledge they have but
also their values.

Here we have the answer to the question: What commanded the faith of John Dewey? The answer is: Dewey's
religious commitment was given to the kind of communication which continuously creates and sustains in being the
human mind and personality, human society and culture and
human history when history means the resources for human
living accumulated by past generations and communicated to
the present.

Immediately someone makes objection thus: What has this to do with religious faith? Even if you call it faith, I do not see anything religious in it. Dewey himself did not discuss it under the head of religion.

I shall endeavor to demonstrate that this faith in communication is not only profoundly religious; it is the substance of the Christian faith and of other faiths also, when you get down to the substance hidden beneath dogma and doctrine. I shall take the Christian faith to illustrate this point.

The center of the Christian faith is the revelation of God in Jesus Christ. The doctrine about this revelation can be stated thus: The power of God unto salvation was revealed in Jesus Christ and is continuously revealed in Jesus Christ, the hope of the world.

We now ask: What was revealed in Jesus Christ which has the power to create, to sustain, to save from evil and transform toward the best that human life can ever attain? What is this revelation? The following statement made by Jesus is often quoted as containing the revelation of God in Jesus Christ: "Whoever has seen me, has seen the Father."

Let us assume for the sake of the argument that this statement was actually made by Jesus and that it is finally authoritative concerning the revelation of God. Many would not accept these assumptions. But for the time being, we are discussing the point with those who appeal to this statement as authoritative and who are convinced that these words represent the substance of what Jesus said in his own Aramaic language.

When Jesus said, "Whoever has seen me, has seen the Father," the word "see" might be taken in the most literal sense. When understood in this way, "to see" means to receive upon the retina of the eye an image produced by light rays reflected from an object. If this were the meaning of the word "see" in the statement made by Jesus, then what the disciples could see was the body of Jesus and nothing more.

Therefore if you understand what Jesus said in this crudely literal sense, his statement comes to this: Whoever has seen this physiological organism of mine has seen the Father because God the Father has a body like mine, same size, same features.

I do not think that anybody interprets the words in this way; and if anybody does, I am sure that the vast majority of Christians would say that he is wrong.

In what sense, then, are we to understand the word "see" when Jesus says, Whoever has seen me, has seen the Father? Surely it means not merely visual perception but rather the experience which the disciples had in association with Jesus. And what was this experience? I think the answer is plain. They experienced a transformation of their lives and character lifting them to a level of power and goodness not otherwise possible. Furthermore, this transformation was caused by the kind of communication they had with Jesus.

If this understanding of the matter is correct, we have an answer to the question, How was God revealed in Jesus Christ and what is the revelation? The revelation was the transforming power of this kind of communication. What then is God as revealed in Jesus Christ? God as revealed in Jesus Christ is the transforming, saving power of this kind of communication which creates appreciative understanding of one another and transmits the values of one to the other.

But this kind of communication was not limited to the physical presence of Jesus. It continued with the disciples after Jesus was gone and was communicated by them to still others to form the early Christian church. Furthermore, the central message of Christianity has been that men are saved by the gospel. But the gospel is a kind of communication. Now to be sure some have seemed to say that this kind of communication must occur in a church and be spoken from a pulpit. But this is plainly false. The kind of communication which Jesus had was not in a church and was not spoken from a pulpit. It occurred as they walked over the countryside on any day of the week.

Some will object further and say that this communication can have this transforming power only if it contain a certain subject matter specified in the form of a set of doctrines. But historic Christianity is split and riven and broken into fragments over the question of which doctrine. Each sect and each division insists that the communication must contain one set of doctrines while all the other divisions of the Christian faith insist that some other doctrine must be included or excluded. Furthermore, all these controversial doctrines claim to go back to the communication which Jesus had with his disciples. But is it not plain that if great scholars and sincere Christians disagree on which of this vast array of diverse doctrines are to be found in the communication which Jesus had with his disciples, it cannot be the case that any of these doctrines are plainly and indubitably contained in his communication? Sincere and scholarly men devoting their entire lives to the study of Jesus could not disagree so radically if any of these doctrines are clearly stated in the communication which Jesus had with his disciples. So we must conclude, the saving power of the communication did not lie in any clear statement of any of these doctrines. Rather the transforming power of the communication must have been in its quality, namely, that quality by which it enabled each to enter into deep appreciative awareness of the individuality of others and thereby acquire from them the values which could be progressively integrated into a depth and fullness of vision transforming their lives.

This kind of communication runs all through human life at some low level. I believe it is always present when human beings are associated and their relations are not entirely mechanized. But there are times when it rises up with great transforming power and that seems to have been the case with Jesus and his disciples.

I do not mean to suggest that Dewey himself looked to Jesus to find this communication commanding his faith. So far as I know, he never did. But I think, if you asked him, he would have agreed that Jesus did communicate with his disciples and that the kind of communication which occurred was of the transforming kind. But regardless of what Dewey thought about the matter, if it be true that the creative and transforming power of a kind of communication commanded Dewey's faith, and if this kind of communication did occur between Jesus and his disciples, then so it is. What Dewey thought on that point is irrelevant.

I do not think that Dewey would call himself a Christian except in the sense of inheriting the Christian tradition like all the rest of us. So far as I know he never belonged to any church nor attended church. He signed the Humanist Manifesto which was a declaration of faith by a group denying that there is any God in the traditional and popular form of that belief. Yet in the little book on *A Common Faith* which is the one book Dewey wrote on religion, he professed belief in God as interpreted by him. But as we shall see, his reference to God is very ambiguous; and in his most explicit statements about the divine presence, I do not think any one, or hardly any one, would accept what he says about God as being acceptable.

The first part of his book on *A Common Faith* is given over to an attack on religion. He wishes to distinguish between doctrines, rituals and institutions called religion and a religious attitude. This attitude, he says, is often distorted if not perverted by these institutional forms of religion. The religious attitude, Dewey makes plain, is necessary to the conduct of human life. The purpose of the book is to rescue this religious attitude from the distortions, perversions and concealments imposed upon it by the institutional forms of religion.

His attack on religion has outraged many good religious

people. I find that many religious people insist that religion is always good. If it is not good, then it is not religion. Dewey took the opposite view. He said that a great deal of religion is evil. Here again may I refer to something which Dewey had in common with Jesus. Probably no one in human history ever blasted with fiercer denunciation the religion of his day than did Jesus. The pharisees were the outstanding exemplars of religion in his time. He said of them that they were whited sepulchers, full of dead men's bones. Dewey never went so far as that in his criticism of religion. But Jesus went even farther. He said to the religious people of his time: Ye generation of vipers, how can you escape from the damnation of hell?

Jesus was not the only one who criticized the religion of his time and place. Amos and the other great Hebrew prophets did also. Martin Luther damned the Christian church of his day which was the Roman Catholic. Many other examples might be cited of great religious personalities denouncing the religion which prevailed round about them.

One can always say that what is called evil religion is false religion, just as one can say that evil in the home is a false home, evil in mother is false mother and that evil in everything which has a good name is falsely given that name. One can do this but he does not change the facts of the case by doing it. The evil is still as evil as ever. Furthermore, this struggle to keep a good name from being smeared by evil is always in danger of concealing and denying the evil in order to protect the good name. Names become deceptive when it is claimed that they always stand for what is good. In such case they are devices by which we conceal the evil in us by giving it a good name.

In discussing this point with good religious people who will not agree that there is evil in their religion, I come around to a final argument which always wins consent. I say, at least you will agree that Wieman's religion is very much in need of being purged and corrected. Good religious people always agree with me on this point. So we end the argument in sweet harmony.

Dewey criticized very severely the religion which he saw round about him. In doing this he was in the company of the great religious personalities of history.

But when we turn to what Dewey actually did in his attempt to criticize and reconstruct religion, one becomes more critical. The kind of religion which he did not throw out of the window, the kind of religion which he kept on the seat beside him, calling it a reformed kind of religious attitude, is what he should have thrown out of the window. This point is so important that I must try to drive it home by telling a story.

An American was traveling in England. He was on one of those trains with little compartments along the side. He could not find a seat. The train was loaded and there were no empty places. He went from one compartment to another and everything was full until he came to a compartment where a woman was sitting with a female dog on the seat beside her. He said to her. Lady, will you not please put that dog down on the floor and let me have that seat? The woman said, No, I bought a ticket for this dog and this seat is reserved for her. The man went back and stood in the aisle for a time but he had broken arches and his feet were hurting him dreadfully. So he went to the woman again and said, Won't you please put the dog on the floor and let me have that seat? My feet are torturing me so that I can hardly endure it. The woman said, No, and looked out of the window. The man went back to the trainmaster to see if he could get some help but the trainmaster could not help him. The woman had bought the ticket for the dog and the seat was reserved.

Finally the man could not stand it any longer. He went to the compartment, picked up the dog and threw it out of the window and sat down. An Englishman was sitting on the seat opposite and had been watching the whole affair. He took his pipe out of his mouth and said to his companion, Americans always do the wrong thing. On the highway driving an automobile they keep to the right instead of the left. At the table they hold their fork in the wrong hand. And now this American has thrown the wrong bitch out of the window.

My point is that Dewey did the wrong thing when he criticized religion. What he threw out of the window he should have kept. And what he sat down beside, he should have thrown out. I shall show that he did make this mistake by examining what he said about the religious attitude in his book *A Common Faith*. On page 27 he writes:

> Any activity pursued in behalf of an ideal end against obstacles and in spite of threats of personal loss because of conviction of its general and enduring value is religious in quality.

Then on page 33 he goes on:

> I should describe this faith as the unification of the self through allegiance to inclusive ideal ends, which imagination presents to us and to which the human will responds as worthy of controlling our desires and choices.

Now let us note what he says about God. Following statements are selected from pages 42 to 51.

> On one score the word [God] can mean only a particular Being. On the other score, it denotes the unity of all ideal ends arousing us to desire and action. . . . Suppose for the moment that the word "God" means the ideal ends that at a given time and place one acknowledges as

having authority over his volition and emotion, the values
to which one is supremely devoted, as far as these ends,
through imagination, take on unity. If we make this sup-
position, the issue will stand out clearly in contrast with
the doctrine of religions that "God" designates some kind
of Being having prior and therefore non-ideal existence.
. . . The idea that "God" represents a unification of ideal
values that is essentially imaginative in origin when the
imagination supervenes in conduct, is attended with verbal
difficulties owing to our frequent use of the word "imagination" to denote fantasy and doubtful reality. But the
reality of ideal ends as ideals is vouched for by their un-
deniable power in action. . . . The unification effected
through imagination is not fanciful, for it is the reflex of
the unification of practical and emotional attitudes. The
unity signifies not a single Being, but the unity of loyalty
and effort evoked by the fact that many ends are one in
the power of their ideal, or imaginative, quality to stir and
hold us.

Dewey explicitly denies that God, as he uses this word, can
be a form of existence. Neither is God eternal Being. God is
not a "Personality having objective existence." (p. 45)
Dewey goes on to write:

The view I have advanced is sometimes treated as if
the identification of the divine with ideal ends left the
ideal wholly without roots in existence and without support from existence. The objection implies that my view
commits one to such a separation of the ideal and the existence that the ideal has no chance to find lodgment even
as a seed that might grow and bear fruit. [In opposition
to this misunderstanding of what I have said] what I have
tried to show is that the ideal itself has its roots in natural
conditions; it emerges when the imagination idealizes ex-

istence by laying hold of the possibilities offered to thought and action. . . . The idealizing imagination seizes upon the most precious things found in the climacteric moments of experience and projects them. . . . They are had, they exist as good, and out of them we frame our ideal ends.

The aims and ideals that move us are generated through imagination. But they are not made out of imaginary stuff. They are made out of the hard stuff of the world of physical and social experience . . . The new vision does not arise out of nothing, but emerges . . . Moreover the process of creation is experimental and continuous. The artist, scientific man, or good citizen, depends upon what others have done before him and are doing around him. The sense of new values that become ends to be realized arises first in dim and uncertain form. As the values are dwelt upon and carried forward in action they grow in definiteness and coherence . . . The process endures and advances with the life of humanity. What one person and one group accomplish becomes the standing ground and starting point of those who succeed them.

These considerations may be applied to the idea of God, or, to avoid misleading conceptions, to the idea of the divine. This idea is, as I have said, one of ideal possibilities unified through imaginative realization and projection. But this idea of God, or of the divine, is also connected with all the natural forces and conditions—including man and human asociation—that promote the growth of the ideal and that further its realization. . . . For there are forces in nature and society that generate and support the ideals.

In these statements about God at least three different references are given the name of "God." First of all God is identified with the ideal, provided that the ideal unifies many values and commands the full allegiance of the individual, thereby unifying his personality under the control of a ruling commitment.

But then he goes on to identify God with something else, namely, that exercise of the imagination by which the ideal and the actual are united. That is to say, ideals become wrought into the actual living of human life. The strivings of men and the processes of society take on a distinctive character because of the ideals which are pursued. This tying of the ideals into the actual processes of the existing world, says Dewey, is the work of imagination; and when imagination operates in this way, the operation is given the name of "God."

But now we come to still a third meaning attached to the word "God" by Dewey. He writes: "This idea of God . . . is also connected with all the natural forces and conditions . . . that promote the growth of the ideal." I underline the words "promote the growth of the ideal."

Here we have three different things, each given the name of God. Two only will here be examined. In the one case, God is the ideal commanding the supreme allegiance of an individual or group at some time and place. But God is also what promotes the growth of the ideal. These two are in conflict in human life. The most bitter and terrible conflicts have arisen between those who give supreme allegiance to a fixed and changeless ideal held to be supreme above all others, and those who are committed to what transforms the ideal, fitting it to the changing demands of changing conditions, different people and new social relations.

We cannot give supreme allegiance to both of these. When they conflict, priority must be given to one over the other. Therefore if the word "God" refers to what should take first priority in human life, supreme over all else, commanding the last devotion and the final obedience, one of these and only one can be identified with God. Is it the ideal taken by itself? Or is it the creativity which more or less continuously transforms the ideal in such a way as to guide human striving toward the greater good when changes occur in nature, in technology, in the personalities involved and in the structure of society?

If we search through the wide expanse of Dewey's writings, I think there can be no doubt about the answer to this question. Dewey is always insisting that the ideal must grow, it must change to meet the changing conditions of life, to fit the needs of different people, different social relations and new situations and, above all, to comprehend and unify a wider range and diversity of values and goal-seeking activities. Perhaps no refrain sounds more continuously in Dewey's work than this.

So we reach the conclusion. If Dewey is going to use the name of God at all within the scope of his discussion, it must be applied to what transforms the ideal in such a way as to guide to the greater good when conditions change.

If this is true, we come to another question which strikes very deep into the issues of human existence. What is this process going on in human life which transforms the ideal in such a way as to guide to the greater good when conditions change? In asking this question we must understand that any such change in the ideal involves also a change in the organization of personality, a change in the order of society and, when the change is momentous, a change in the course of history. Therefore when we ask this question we are probing very deeply into what determines the destiny of man.

If we are to keep our inquiry within the confines of Dewey's thinking in seeking an answer to this question, we must turn back to what Dewey said about communication. He stated that there is a kind of communication to be distinguished from all other kinds, which creates appreciative understanding of the unique individuality of persons and peoples and which, in consequence, endows each with values, insights, capacities derived from the other; and which, further, integrates these diverse values into a comprehensive unity after they have been criticized and evaluated, so that the participant individuals have a deeper community with one another, a greater abundance of value in their lives, with capacity to cooperate more effectively for a greater good; and have an ideal shared in common which comprehends more of the values of life than any ideal possessed by the parties before they engaged in this kind of communication.

All of us, whether we recognize it or not, have experienced this kind of communication to some degree. Everyone who has a happy marriage, has undergone this kind of transformation by way of communication which is subtle, intimate and continuous. Everyone who has lived intimately and lovingly with a small child has experienced this kind of communication, the child learning from you and you from the child, each transforming the other. In so far as there is any community here in the United States, made up of diverse peoples from the ends of the earth, it has been created by this kind of communication. There is, to be sure, a superficial conformity, a superimposed pattern, suppressing and killing appreciation of individuality. But that is not the only thing which has happened to the people who make up the community called the people of the United States. Beneath conformity to a superimposed pattern there is at a deeper level a true community. Otherwise there would be no power and no virtue in what we call our country.

What I have said about the United States applies also to India, made up originally of peoples of the most diverse kinds, streaming into that country from different regions. The same can be said of all the great historic communities which ever existed. The same will also be said of a world community if ever it comes into existence; and eventually it must come into existence if the human race is to be saved from irremediable disaster.

Subtly, silently, in ways which are mostly hidden and unconscious, there occurs between human beings when they are associated, a kind of communication which operates beneath the cruelty, beneath the indifference, beneath the exploitation and the arrogance, beneath the superimposed conformity. This deeper, hidden kind of communication creates community. It creates some appreciative understanding of one another whereby each learns from the other, not knowledge primarily, although this is included, but even more the values cherished by the other person or people. This deeper communication, often hidden but potent, it alone can save us and it alone can make us human.

This kind of communication operates almost continuously in subtle and hidden ways. But there are times when it rises up, becomes dominant, powerful, radically transforming. As said before, in our Western tradition the one great historic instance of this kind of communication rising to such dominance over counter processes was the transformation wrought by Jesus and his disciples. In consequence, this manifestation of saving and transforming power has been called the revelation of God in Jesus Christ.

Dewey frequently denied that any one principle can be the moral guide of human conduct. But he suggests in many places that intelligence should always seek to release goal-seeking activities in widest range and variety. Furthermore, he says this is accomplished by innovating insights emerging when engaged in solving problems. This is very much like creativity expanding the horizons of life, to use our own expression.

Dewey's use of the word "God" presents a problem which cannot be evaded in this context. The problem is this: When and how and in reference to what should this word "God" be used? The problem is much more serious and difficult than appears upon the surface. It is serious and difficult because many people speak religiously of God but never specify what they mean when they use the word. Many insist that you cannot specify what is meant and should not attempt to do so. "You cannot define God," they say. God is infinite and no finite mind can state what God is. Consequently the word is used without anybody knowing just what is meant. It is even proclaimed, in a recent book to which all the ranking theologians of our country contributed, that the theologians whose business it is to study this problem are more or less agreed that no statement can be made or should be made which presumes to characterize the being of God. I quote from the book mentioned.

> . . . the realities apprehended in religious faith exceed the powers of the human mind and human speech to describe and define hence there is skepticism regarding *all* "definitions" of God. Positively, this encourages recourse to symbolic representations of trans-rational realities through the employment of "myth." [3]

Is this the right answer to our question? Must we repudiate all attempts to specify the kind of being to which reference is made when we speak religiously of God? Must we be content to say that God is a trans-rational reality?

If this policy is adopted disastrous evils ensue. When the word "God" is used without specifying the distinguishing characteristics of the being referred to, the word becomes a device concealing from others and from ourselves the true character of the faith which motivates our lives. Consequently when the word is used in this way, it becomes a device by which we give sanctity to our goals of endeavor no matter how unworthy they may be. The word becomes a cover to protect us from criticism and correction because no one can criticize or correct God.

Of course when one uses the word in this way to refer to mystery, to trans-rational reality and to uncomprehended being which the human mind cannot characterize, he must still conform to the social pattern like everybody else. If he steals or kills or does anything else which outrages his associates, he will be punished. He must act in conformity to what the culture permits. But within these limits, he can make himself think and others think that he lives for God and with God, no matter how superficial may be the faith by which he lives. In such case, religion takes on the form of great evil. This has happened very often in human history and in the lives of individuals.

This is reason for rejecting the answer to our question which is given by the leading theologians of our time. Remember the question is this: What kind of being do we designate when we use the word God? The most famous and influential theologian in the United States, Paul Tillich, says that the word "God," when it points to man's ultimate concern, does not refer to any *kind* of being whatsoever. Man's ultimate concern, he says, is the ground of all being and this is utterly beyond all powers of the human mind to know. No distinction or characterization whatsoever can be applied to it. As I have just stated, when one uses the word in this way, all the evils come flocking in which I have just described.

There are many today who say that we should abandon the use of the word "God" in serious religious discourse because it leads to endless controversy or else to the deceptive devices I have just portrayed. This claim that we should repudiate the use of the word calls for examination. Perhaps John Dewey, after the misunderstanding aroused by his use of the word, might agree that it should not be used when discourse intends to be intelligent.

It is true that use of this word causes confusion, hypocrisy, self deception and often brings thinking to a dead stop. All these evils should be recognized. But there is another side to the problem and this other side is of utmost importance.

We must have some way to indicate what should be given first priority in the lives of all men to the end of their salvation from self defeat and self destruction. This necessity can be stated in a few simple propositions. Human life must have diversity else we suffer intolerable frustration. But diverse ways of life equipped with annihilating power lead to irremediable disaster unless all concerned give first priority to what creates community in the midst of diversity. Therefore we cannot be saved unless we all commit ourselves in religious faith to what operates in human life to create and sustain unique individuality and diverse ways of life but does it in such a way as to create at the same time community and appreciative understanding between these unique individuals and diverse ways of life. As the power of man increases by leaps and bounds, while at the same time the bonds of interdependence grow tighter and closer, so that we block and frustrate one another if we do not have community and appreciative understanding of one another, we move toward that hour when the destiny of man will be determined fatefully. The great hope of the future is not the economic abundance and leisure, the good health and long life, provided by science and technology. The great hope of the future is that men will be forced in the presence of a horror they cannot face, to give first priority to providing the conditions under which creative communication can create community amidst the diversities of life. If that time ever comes, a goodness will spread over the face of the planet such as never was before. If that time does not come, a darkness will spread.

Now there is no other word except "God," or some synonym thereof, which points imperatively to what should be given first place in the lives of all men universally whereby they may be saved from destruction and transformed toward the greater good. We must have some kind of language, some verbiage, by which to make plain to the minds of men this stark reality involved in human existence. The stark reality is the life and death necessity of having diversity combined with a process of interchange creating community.

It is not enough to point out negatively what should *not* be given the place of God. Neither is it enough to say that God is an incomprehensible mystery. Both of these procedures, when taken by themselves alone, point straight down the road of disaster. We must have some way of stating positively what must be given sovereignty over all human life to save it from the path of no return. If there is some other language which can say this imperatively and can be understood to this effect by people generally, wherein the word "God" or its synonyms do not appear, such language might be used. But no other language is now available. The language about God, referring to what creates, sustains, saves and transforms toward the greater good, commanding our supreme allegiance above all else, is so deep-laid and far-flung in our culture and in most of the cultures of the world, that I do not believe any other kind of language can be effective. By effective is not meant merely emotional. Effective here means to make plain a fact which must be recognized else we cannot be saved.

It is true that this language of religion in the minds of many carries with it the connotation of supernatural beings. With others it conveys the sense of a glamorous mystery. For still others it brings to mind a miscellaneous assortment of superstitions and prejudices. But along with the supernaturalism, the glamorous mystery and the superstition, the language is always intended to refer to what creates, sustains, saves and transforms. Furthermore, it is the language of commitment and passionate devotion. To substitute for it the language of criticism employed by intellectuals who stand on the side-lines and talk about the folly and error of men, but have nothing grandly and passionately positive to say, is to talk the language of death. It is the language of death because these sophisticated critics will be swept over the precipice by the buffalo herd which has enough passion in it to get things done, whether for good or evil. Criticism has its place but they who are critics and nothing more, are dawdling diddlers to be pushed out of the way when the passions of life and death begin to surge. Without the word "God" the ultimate passion and the supreme devotion, not of the individual or the group, but of all mankind in the total stream of history, cannot be expressed by the Western mind.

Now you may ask, what has this to do with Dewey's faith? It has everything to do with it. Dewey raised this question about the use of the word into clear consciousness and made it a central question of dispute. This he did because of the controversy which his usage aroused, because of the motive which led him to use the word, namely, to express man's supreme allegiance, and his later regret that he had used it. Furthermore, the most intelligent people of our time are being divided into two opposing groups, one group insisting that religious commitment must be to God, the other group repudiating that expression entirely. This division and opposition should not continue if mankind is to find its way to a guiding and sustaining commitment. Hence it is a problem which should not be ignored nor evaded and it is a problem which Dewey's faith cast into the arena of public debate.

So, in considering the ambiguities involved in Dewey's statement about his faith, we are forced to examine this problem. To what should we refer when we speak of God?

To answer that question we should go first of all to the Christian tradition because the word as we use it acquires its meaning from this tradition. People who inherit other traditions will go to their traditions to find the meaning of the words they use; but for us the word "God" acquires its meaning from the Christian and Jewish tradition, like all other words in our religious language.

In the Christian and Jewish tradition certain doings are ascribed to God. Five of these are outstanding. First of all God is creator. Therefore one kind of doing which distinguishes God is the doing of creativity. Second, a further doing distinguishing God is the doing of salvation. Third, God is the judge and ruler of history. In the fourth place, God is the being revealed in Jesus Christ. Finally, God works in the church in the form of the Holy Spirit when the church is faithful in its mission.

Here are five kinds of doing ascribed to God, the doing of creativity, the doing of salvation, the doing which creates and sustains history and keeps it going, the doing revealed in Jesus Christ and the doing of the Holy Spirit through the church.

Can we find any such five-fold operation going on in human life and history? I claim that we can. Furthermore, this five-fold operation is precisely the kind of communication we have been describing, the kind which creates appreciative understanding of the individuality of persons and peoples when they allow it to operate in their lives, creating society, sustaining all these in being and increasing the values in them, when required conditions are present. This operative presence creates in each individual his capacity to love and appreciate and understand the individuality of others.

God is not only the creator of man. He is the creator of the world when the world means everything which the cognitive powers of man can know. This kind of communication creates and expands our cognitive powers and in this way, relative to those cognitive powers, it creates the world, that is to say, all that we are able to know.

So much for God the creator. Now look at God the

savior. To save means to transform man as he cannot transform himself, to deliver him from evil and bring him to the greatest good which human life can ever attain. Here again it can be demonstrated that when men are transformed in this way it is because the kind of communication here considered has risen up with power sufficient to make them aware that they are profoundly appreciated in respect to their own true individuality and have like appreciation of some other one or more. This sense of being profoundly appreciated and understood and this capacity to appreciate and understand the other, so that each is endowed with the values of the other and each can be his true self and understand himself as he could not do before, this is what saves man. This is what transforms a man from the evil to the good.

A dramatic portrayal of salvation in this way is presented in Ibsen's play *Peer Gynt*. You may remember that Peer traveled all over the world doing all manner of evil and foolish things, in order to "succeed." He pretended to be this kind of person and that, anything to succeed with his idea of success. At last, an old man, he comes home to Solveig who has loved him all these years and understands him better than anyone else. As he comes home he meets what corresponds to the devil who tells him that he will be damned if he does not recover the individuality which God intended him to be. In the presence of Solveig he cries out: Where is Peer Gynt with God's seal upon his brow? Where, where is he? And Solveig answers: I can answer that question. Where is Peer Gynt with God's seal upon his brow? In my faith, in my hope, in my love. And Peer Gynt is saved.

This is fiction. It is drama. But it tells us the truth about human beings and the way of their salvation. Not that a woman's love can save necessarily. But when men are saved from the evil ways of life it is because they find this kind of appreciative understanding somewhere and in some way.

This brings us to the third kind of doing which distinguishes God from everything else. It is the doing which creates and sustains history and keeps it going and which judges history in the sense of cutting it down when it goes far wrong.

History means the consequences of past events so far as they reach into the present to shape our lives and make us what we are. The consequences of past events cannot reach into the present to shape our lives and make us what we are except by way of that kind of communication which transmits these consequences from person to person, from generation to generation and from age to age. Without this kind of communication, there could be no history because the consequences of past events could not reach us. History as thus understood is not merely our knowledge of past events. Rather it is the consequences of past events in so far as these consequences shape our lives today, whether we know anything about them or not. History is the creation and transmission of a culture, preeminently the language with all its meanings. This language with all its meanings is created in each child and youth and in each individual throughout his life by the kind of communication which transmits from one to the other the values, the knowledge, the skill, the ideals, the memories composing the culture of that time and place.

When this kind of comunication sinks to a low level then the stream of history sinks to a low level. That is to say, fewer of the values, and less of all the consequences of the past, can reach the present. In such case, the present begins to move toward a period called the dark ages, because less of all the resources for human living created in the past can reach the present. In this way God judges history and condemns it, when men do not allow God to operate fully and effectively in their lives. This is so, if the doing of God in human life is identified with the kind of communication we are here considering.

If we accept the meaning which the Jewish Christian tradition has given to the word "God," namely the doing which creates and sustains history and judges history, then God must be identified with this kind of communication.

But how about the revelation of God in Jesus Christ? That question has already been answered. Also it was previously shown that this transforming and saving power of communication continued after Jesus' death in the fellowship of the disciples which formed the early church. It became the mission of the church to transmit it at that high level of dominance over counter processes where it can exercise saving power over these other processes going on in human life. This has been called the Holy Spirit.

So we find our answer to the question, to what should we refer when we use the word "God"? We should refer to that kind of doing which is ascribed to God, namely, the doing of creation; the doing of salvation; the doing which keeps history going and judges history, the doing revealed in Jesus Christ; and, finally, the doing which occurs in the church when it is faithful to its mission.

But this kind of doing, in all five of the different forms, is the doing of a kind of communication. This kind of communication occurs to some degree between persons all the time. Without it we would not be human. But to be radically creative, transforming and saving, it must rise to a high level of dominance over counter processes which in ordinary life suppress and obstruct it. When the required conditions are present, however, it does rise to a level of power endowing human life with all its great values.

Different people apply different tests to any being under consideration to ascertain if it should be given the name of God. These tests can be put in the form of questions thus: (1) Does the being under consideration conform to the mental picture of God held by the individual or group? This is like saying that the name "United States" cannot be given to the government and people of this country unless they conform to the mental picture of them in the mind of the Fourth of July patriot. Plainly such a test inevitably falsifies. (2) Is the being ontologically prior to every other being in the sense that everything in existence and possibility depends upon it? This test ignores the primary concern of the founders of the great religions. These founders were primarily concerned with what can save man from his evil ways and bring him to the best which life can attain. They were interested in ontology only in a very secondary way. (3) Does the being operate in human life to save man from evil and bring him to the best when required conditions are met? This human test generally conflicts with the ontological one. This being discovered by ontological and metaphysical inquiry does not manifestly operate to save and transform man unless the evidence is doctored to make it appear to do so. Such being the case, honesty requires decision for one of the other. Many try to evade the decision by covering the contradiction with metaphor, poetic symbol and dogma which cannot be taken to mean what it says.

Religious language as it prevails today is a tangle of ambiguities, illusions, diverse and unanalyzed meanings. All kinds of people with all sorts of purposes use religious words, each putting his own meaning into them and often himself not knowing what he intends when he speaks religiously. The leading theologians do not help because they themselves reduce religious language to myth and symbol, defending this practice on the ground that we must deal with realities beyond the reach of rational understanding. No free faith and no common faith can ever be had in this way because there is no escape from domination by religious leaders if we cannot know what it is to which we give ourselves in ultimate commitment. If we cannot know, we can only be swept along by the religious appeal of myth and symbol without knowing what deadly cataract is ahead to dash us against the rocks. We must know, in language correctly descriptive, what it is to which we give ourselves in religious devotion to be transformed by it as we cannot transform ourselves.

A faith not based on descriptive truth cannot give us freedom and cannot save us. The hard realities descriptively known must sustain us else we cannot be sustained. The soft mire of symbolism, of convictions unsustained by evidence derived from observation of what happens when we follow them, of myths and metaphors which cannot be translated into designated structures of existence, all this is the mire sucking us down.

It is easy to say: Let the jungle stand uncleared and undrained, with the mire in the middle of it. Many good and pious people will be grateful to you for not disturbing the faith sustained by uninterpreted symbolism. Also many highly intellectual people will approve of you if you keep the symbols pointing into mystery and nothing more, because they like that sort of thing. They are then free to interpret the symbols as they like without being criticized and without the need to tell anyone how they use them. So likewise if you let the jungle stand undisturbed, you will be approved by people who do not want to be bothered by religion. So long as it continues to be a jungle, they can ignore it. So, if you do nothing about the jungle of religious language, if you let it stand as it is, you will be approved and honored and may live a happy life. But John Dewey will not go along.

CHAPTER THREE

PERSONALISM ANSWERS

Perhaps the most obvious point of disagreement between John Dewey's naturalism and personalism concerns the personality of God. One of the central teachings of personalism is that God is a person.

If God exercises any power different in kind from the powers exercised by man, then God is not a person when "personality" refers to the essential characteristics distinguishing the human being from everything else. If God exercises powers greater than human but none different in kind, it can be said that God is a person. But if any of God's powers are different in kind from those essential to the being of human personality, then God cannot be a person. It is a logical fallacy to call God a person if any of his essential powers are different in kind from those essential to, and definitive of, the human being. This is so because the established meaning of the word "personality" is to designate the characteristics which are distinctive and essential to the human being.

Consider an analogy. A square is still a square, no matter

how big it is; but a square is not a circle. Square and circle have many features in common. Both are spatial, both are plane figures, both enclose space by a continuous line. But no matter how many features are identical in respect to the two, a square is not a circle if there is any one feature essential and definitive for the circle which is not essential and definitive for the square.

Now all this applies to God and man. No matter how many features one may claim to be the same in God and in man, differing only in magnitude, if there is any one characteristic essential to the being of God which is different from what is essential to the being of man, then God is not a person any more than a square is a circle.

The personalists attribute to God a power essential to, and definitive of, the being of God which is different from any power essential to, and definitive of, the being of man. Professor Bertocci so states in an article published in *Philosophy and Phenomenological Research*, issue of December, 1956. On page 220 it is asserted that God "in creating uses no means co-eternal with himself." But no human being ever creates anything without using some means pre-existing before he himself existed. In other words, no human being creates *ex nihilo*. But God does, according to the teaching of personalism. Professor Bertocci admits this difference between God and man. Furthermore, he admits that it presents a difficulty in the teaching of personalism. Nevertheless he insists that God is a personality even though God exercises this power which is different in kind from any power exercised by man. He protects himself in affirming this self contradictory statement by calling it a mystery.

This appeal to mystery to protect a self contradictory statement is a common practice in theological circles now dominant. But the theologians who do this repudiate the tests of reason when it comes to the farther reaches of faith. Personalism, I am glad to say, does not repudiate these tests in matters of religious doctrine. Hence Professor Bertocci contradicts himself when he says that God is a personality while at the same time attributing to God a power essential to, and definitive of, God which cannot be essential to, and definitive of, personality. His statements are as contrary as to say that a square is a circle.

This argument against the belief that God is a person is based on a presupposition of personalism, namely, that God creates *ex nihilo*. This presupposition is not shared by religious naturalism. Nevertheless it is important to note that personalism cannot defend its belief in the personality of God without becoming involved in a self-contradiction. There are other reasons for denying that God can be a person. These will now be examined.

Personality is progressively created. Beginning with conception this development is biological. After birth the biological development is supplemented by a process over and above the biological. This process which creates beyond the biological, but not independently of it, is a kind of interchange between the infant and those who care for it. This interchange creates in the developing child the level distinctively human. This level distinctively human is most conspicuously characterized by the use of syntactical language.

The kind of interchange creating progressively the level distinctively human has two aspects. First it creates in the child an appreciative understanding of the thoughts, feelings, attitudes and intentions of his associates as these are conveyed by language and other signs. Secondly, it integrates into his own unique individuality the diversities and nuances and wide ranges of meaning carried by the language of his culture. This process in the form of interchange and in the form of internal integration creates progressively the personality of the child so far as his thoughts, feelings and habits are derived from the culture in which he lives. We know that this creativity occurs in human life after this manner although we have not penetrated into the depth and complexity of it and we need to know more about it. But the reality of it can scarcely be doubted.

This understanding of the way personality comes into existence should make plain that God cannot be a personality and at the same time exercise the powers attributed to God. The argument is as follows. If God is a personality and if the word "personality" designates what is essential to, and definitive of, the human being, then God must be progressively created from a sub-human level by interchange with other persons; and these other persons must exist before God can be created by interchange with them. Human beings have been progressively created by this kind of interchange, beginning two hundred thousand years ago more or less. It began with some kind of sub-human animal rising to the human level.

In looking at this creativity progressively creating the human personality we shall ignore the development of the biological organism. This is, of course, in the picture but personalists deny that God has a biological organism. Therefore, we omit the biological aspect of the matter and consider only the thinking, feeling, imagining and other spiritual activities which are essential to the human personality. These spiritual activities are progressively created after the manner just described.

"Spiritual activities" is a very vague term and we must have something definite before us in considering this problem. So, to understand specifically what we are discussing, five of these spiritual activities can be examined.

The first of these five aspects of spiritual life progressively created to form the human personality is expanding the range of what the individual can know, and can control, can appreciate as good and distinguish as evil.

The second of the five is the deepening and correcting of the appreciative understanding of oneself and of other persons. Adding the word "appreciative" to "understanding" is intended to signify that the understanding includes discriminating evaluation.

The third aspect of personality progressively created is a progressive unifying or integration of all its acquisitions. The integration must be progressive because new developments of the personality are always arising and these must be integrated into the individuality of the person, else they generate disruptive inner conflicts in the form of neuroses, psychoses and other mental ills.

The fourth aspect of personality progressively created is capacity to undergo failure, defeat, suffering, loss and guilt in such a way that their consequences will be creative and not destructive. The experience of failure, defeat, suffering, guilt and loss is creative when it expands the range of what the individual can know, control, appreciate as good and distinguish as evil; when it deepens his appreciative understanding of himself and of others; when it brings new developments of experience into a firmer and more powerful integration of personality. In other words, failure and suffering are met creatively when they result in the progressive creation of the other aspects of personality.

Finally, the fifth aspect of personality progressively created is freedom. The idea of freedom will be discussed in later chapters.

The process of creating progressively these five aspects of personality is psychological, social and historical. It is historical because this progressive creation requires the accumulation of a culture and a language through a sequence of many generations, each generation adding some increment until a fully developed language and other cultural resources have been acquired in sufficient quantity and quality to make it possible for the level distinctively human to arise.

Here we see the essential features of personality progressively created in each individual from earliest infancy.

With this understanding of personality, can we say that God is a personality?

If God is a person he must be progressively created by interchange between many individuals existing before he can exist; and these individuals previously existing must themselves gradually reach the level of fully developed personality by way of a creativity which can operate effectively only when there is a language and other cultural resources requisite to the human level of life. This language and these other cultural resources must, in turn, have been developed by way of a long sequence of generations, beginning with an organism not yet fully human.

Now if we say that God is a personality, we are saying that God is a creature brought into existence by a creativity ontologically prior to himself. But such a statement contradicts one of the essential characteristics of God. One of the definitive characteristics of God according to personalism is that he be not originally a creature but the original creator. Therefore if we say that God is a personality we again become involved in a self contradiction. We again are saying that a square is a circle.

This brings us to the point where we must examine more carefully this creativity to see how it is related to personality. It operates between persons in the form of a kind of interchange between them. Also it operates throughout history. It also operates in persons in the form of a progressive integration. These three aspects of it, the historical, the interpersonal, and the inner personal are equally essential to it. Creativity is, thus, a process which personality undergoes as it is being progressively created. But creativity in this sense is not anything done by personality. This statement will be confusing unless we distinguish carefully between two kinds of creativity, which is to say two meanings of this word. Certainly human beings can be creative, but the creativity which man does is different from the creativity he undergoes in being progressively created. These two meanings of the word must be distinguished if we are to understand the difference between the creativity of God operating as no personality can operate, and the creativity of man which *is* an operation characteristic of personality.

When a process produces an outcome which the man does not intend, this outcome is not the doing of the man. Only if a process in which a man is involved produces an outcome which he intends to produce, can we say that this outcome is what the man does. On the other hand, if the outcome is not anything which the man can foresee or imagine until after it comes into existence, then its coming into existence is not his doing because he did not intend to produce it.

A few examples of this creativity which personality can undergo but which cannot be the doing of personality are the following. A man undergoes transformation enabling him to imagine and appreciate an ideal when, prior to this transformation, it was entirely outside the bounds of his imagination. Since he could not imagine it before it entered his consciousness, he could not have intended to attain it. Another example is an insight emerging of such sort that it could not emerge until after the individual underwent a reorganization of his personality. Since the insight was inaccessible to him prior to its emergence, it could not have been intended. Consider still another example of this creativity which cannot ever be done by personality because the outcome cannot be intended. A person undergoes a transformation whereby he becomes able to forgive as he could not do and could not want to do, before he underwent the change. Still another example is the case of a person undergoing a transformation whereby he comes to love persons or people whom he did not intend to love but rather intended to hate, prior to the interchange producing this new attitude. A recent movie called *The Defiant Ones*, shows a Negro and a white man bound together with handcuffs and trying to escape the police. At first they are bitter enemies but the interchange between them transforms them, contrary to their intent, into devoted friends ready to sacrifice life and liberty for one another. This is creative interchange.

Since creativity, of the kind here under consideration, operates to produce outcomes which cannot be intended, this kind of creativity cannot be the doing of personality.

It is true that a man may intend to have creativity occur, and to that end may work to provide the conditions conducive to his own creative transformation. But he cannot intend the new insight, the new capacity to forgive, the new love, the new ideal, because these are entirely beyond the reach of his imagination and appreciation until after he has been transformed creatively. He can intend the creativity but he cannot intend the specific nature of what the creativity will produce.

As said before, there is another meaning of the word "creativity," and when this meaning is given to the word, man is creative. A man is creative when he strives to actualize an ideal which he has already imagined. He is creative when he develops the implication of an insight which has already entered his awareness. He is creative when he constructs something according to a new design which has already come within the reach of his imagination. This new design may be a work of art or a new utility; it may be a new way to organize society or conduct the life of the family or introduce some other innovation. But a man can do nothing unless he intends to do it, either consciously or subconsciously. No man can intend to produce an outcome so long as that outcome is beyond the reach of his imagination and beyond the reach of all his powers of apprehension.

Here we have two kinds of creativity. One is a characteristic doing of the human person. The other is what personality undergoes but cannot do. This second kind of creativity is what progressively creates personality in community. If God is identified with this second kind of creativity, then God cannot be a personality. Otherwise stated, if there is a creativity producing what personality cannot produce, then this creativity cannot be personality. We have seen that there is such a creativity and we have seen that it is the kind of doing attributed to God. So we reach the conclusion that God cannot be a personality.

Personalists may reply to this argument after this fashion. Yes, God certainly creates what lies beyond the reach of human imagination but it does not follow that it lies beyond the reach of God's imagination. If the personalist makes this reply he is again denying that God has a characteristic essential to, and definitive of personality. This essential characteristic is the capacity to undergo creative transformation in the sense of acquiring further reaches of imagination never had before; acquiring new insights, more profound appreciative understanding of self and others, in sum, undergoing progressive creation of his own personality in the five kinds of spiritual activity previously listed.

If God does not have this capacity to undergo creative transformation, then he cannot be a personality. If, on the other hand, he can undergo this creativity, then he cannot exercise the power of creativity producing in the personality outcomes beyond the reach of his imagination and intention. Therefore either God exercises the power of creativity progressively creating personality, in which case he cannot be a personality because he is then exercising the creativity no person can exercise but can only undergo; or else, if he is a personality, he is himself the creature of this creativity. A god who is a creature of an ontologically prior creativity is properly called an idol.

This divine creativity, different from the creativity exercised by personality, can be called God if the word "God" refers not to a person but to what creates personality progressively when required conditions are present; creates the world relative to this progressively created mind of man; sustains man as he cannot sustain himself; saves man from evil as he cannot save himself; transforms man so that he can forgive and love and appreciate what he could not by any intentional striving on his own part; endows man with all the spiritual activities previously listed under five heads. This holds true regardless of how much this creativity may differ from the mental picture men have fashioned to represent deity. These imaginary pictures representing God as a person need not necessarily be condemned, if it is understood that they are noncognitive symbols pointing to a creativity which they do not describe. Correct description always falls short of comprehending the full reality of the most important matters, and this is most markedly true of deity. Therefore we very properly use symbols to represent the uncomprehended fullness of the reality beyond the reach of correct description. This practice becomes pernicious and idolatrous when no correct description is recognized or permitted. This pernicious and idolatrous use of symbolism is a common practice in religion and is being viciously promoted by much modern theology.

One of the great virtues of personalism appears in dealing with this question. Personalists have always insisted that if the word "God" is used at all, it should refer to some being accessible to correct description. They reject the use of symbols when these symbols seem to refer to a being while at the same time refusing to specify any characteristics whereby this being can be distinguished from what it is not. By rejecting this use of symbols and setting up specifications, the personalists expose themselves to criticism, but this is the only way that the truth can ever be attained. The dominant theologians of our time win wide acceptance by refusing to specify the kind of being to which their symbols refer and even deny that any such specification is possible. This renders inquiry futile and knowledge impossible but this obscurantism is concealed through the use of symbols seeming to specify when they do not. Over against all this the personalists should be honored even though one disagrees with their specifications.

This completes the criticism of the central doctrine of personalism. It is the claim that God is a person. Another teaching of this religious philosophy calls for criticism. It appears in a statement made by Professor Bertocci in his *Introduction to the Philosophy of Religion*. "The essence or core of religion is the personal belief that one's most important values are sponsored by, or in harmony with, the enduring structure of the universe . . ."

Criticism is directed to the claim that the enduring structure of the universe can sponsor the most important values.

What is called the enduring structure of the universe at any given period in the development of human thought is nothing more than a selection from innumerable structures to be found in the totality of all being. The structure of the universe known to us at any one time is that structure rendered accessible by the hypotheses, the observational data and the mathematical formulations developed up to that time. Another structure of the universe will be discovered when the requisite hypotheses and mathematical formulations and other resources for inquiry become available.

For the moment I do not want to become involved in the metaphysical problem about whether all structures ever to be discovered are eternally in being, or whether inquiry creates the structure, as John Dewey asserts, or whether a third position holds, which is my own. In any case, creative transformation occurs when new structures enter the reach of human imagination, human knowledge and appreciation; and this is a transformation of the human mind and personality. It is also a transformation of human society and culture. Finally it is a transformation of the universe as known to man.

In all three of these dimensions it is a creative transformation.

When the Ptolemaic structure of the universe was supplanted by the Copernican, men suffered acute religious distress because they thought the Ptolemaic structure was the enduring structure and that it sponsored their highest values. Consequently they were ready to burn to death anyone so subversive as to endanger these highest values by claiming that the structure of the universe was not what it seemed. This is the predicament into which men fall when they look to "the enduring structure of the universe" to sponsor their highest values. The conflict between science and theology along with religious bitterness, hate and fear, have arisen out of this error, namely, to look to "the enduring structure of the universe to sponsor our highest values." To escape all this evil, error and illusion, we must look to creativity itself to sponsor our highest values.

But if we look to creativity to sponsor our highest values, the expression "our highest values" must be interpreted to mean not the values which we happen at the present time to esteem highly. Rather our "highest values" must be understood to refer to those values which at present we are not able to appreciate but which will come within the reach of our imagination and appreciation as we undergo creative transformation. More correctly, the highest value is this creativity itself.

Not only does the structure of the universe undergo transformation relative to our knowledge, but also the structure of human personality is transformed creatively. Therefore our highest values must be sought and found not in the structure of the universe and not in the demands of our own personalities as they are now structured and not in our highest ideals. If we seek our highest values in any of these, the outcome will be frustration, disillusion, hate and fear and very probably self destruction, since man now has such enormous power to apply in the service of his illusions. Only by seeking our highest values in creativity can we be saved from these major evils.

The point of all this is not that structures discovered at different periods in man's cultural development are illusions, although it is an illusion to say that any of them is the enduring structure of the universe. Illusions and errors certainly occur; but apart from error and apart from illusion, the structures discovered by different individuals and in different periods of cultural development cannot be called illusions merely on the ground that they differ. They differ because different hypotheses are used. When an hypothesis is confirmed, the structure exposed by it is truly in being, even though some other hypothesis might expose a different structure. Perhaps the great majority of hypotheses have failed to meet the tests of truth. But those which have met the tests are true within the limits of their application. Or, more correctly stated, that statement is true which correctly describes the configuration of data exposed by the hypothesis. But other configurations can be exposed by the application of other theories, and statements correctly describing these configurations are also true.

To illustrate the point, take a very simple example. Suppose a small child has never been outside the nursery. If it could correctly describe the structure of the nursery within some frame of reference, it would be true to say that this was the structure of the universe within the limits of what the child was able to discover. Furthermore, this would be an eternal truth about the universe, namely, that this was the ultimate structure within reach of the child's cognitive powers.

The child in this example is not very different from the adult in the year 1960. The cultural development of man has only just begun. If we do not see that we ourselves are like the child in this respect, we fail to see ourselves as others will see us ten thousand years from now, assuming that civilization is not destroyed in the meantime.

We have no reason whatsoever to think that in this year of 1960 all the structures ever to be discovered have been exposed by the theories thus far used by men in conducting inquiry. Furthermore we are not even justified in thinking that all the structures which have been exposed and will be exposed could ever form a coherent system and so be called a universe. Rather I think the evidence points in the opposite direction. The infinity of possible structures which might be discovered do not form a universe, that is to say, they do not cohere to form a single system. This corresponds with the claim of many great thinkers that ultimate being cannot be characterized in any way because it is without limit and transcends every system which might ever be discovered by the most comprehensive theory.

I repeat, the point of all this is not to say that truth changes. The assertion that truth changes is a self contradictory affirmation. A truth is a statement correctly describing a structure in being which the resources of the culture have made it possible for men to discover. That other structures will be discovered and that this structure first discovered will take on a different character when combined with these others, does not militate against the truth of the first discovery. Ptolemy's theory was not false and neither was Newton's. So likewise other theories which have revolutionized and will revolutionize our view of the universe are true. They are true if they are consistent and comprehend all the data relevant to the theory.

Neither am I saying that truth is relative in the sense that whatever a people in a given culture happen to believe must be accepted as true. Nothing can be accepted as true unless it meets the tests distinguishing a true statement from one that is false. Just what is the method for distinguishing the true from the false need not concern us at this point. Whatever the method may be, there are many possible structures and every statement is true which correctly states what they are. Which of these structures men are able to discover when they correctly distinguish true statements from those that are false, depends upon the hypotheses which are used, the observational data available and whatever other resources for inquiry the culture at that time and place may provide.

If all this is true, the universe as we now know it is a transitory thing, changing and passing away like a cloud in the sky, as human culture undergoes transformation. This does not mean that the universe as we know it lacks reality. It is truly real. It is as real as the cloud in the sky. But to commit our values to the passing cloud under the illusion that it is the enduring structure of the universe is an obvious error. This is the error in personalism when it identifies religion with the belief that our highest values are sponsored by the enduring structure of the universe. Personalism is also in error where it claims to know what the enduring structure is. This error becomes more serious when it is claimed that we discover God by searching out the basic structure of the universe now known to us. When we do this, God becomes as ephemeral as the passing cloud, and just as unreliable.

So long as the word "universe" preserves its identity of meaning through all the changes which the form of the universe may undergo, there must be an enduring structure in the sense of an identity of meaning. This is a tautology and so cannot be disputed. But this does not inform us concerning what this enduring structure may be. If we are to find any identity running through all the changes occurring in the structures attributed to the universe through the ages, it must be the identity of that creativity expanding the range of what the human mind can know, can control, can appreciate as good and distinguish as evil. But this creativity operates in human life, in human history and the mind of man. It cannot be identified with what we now call the universe.

When new structures enter human experience they are creative of the world when the world means all that the human being can know, appreciate or distinguish in any way. They are also creative of the human mind and personality, whether the new structures arise in science or art or in social organization or social convention or in the form of better understanding of oneself and of other persons. Therefore the entry of new structures into human experience, here called creativity, brings on a creative transformation of man and his universe, provided that the new structure is integrated into a system with other structures accepted as true.

Previously John Dewey's view was mentioned. It is that human inquiry creates the new structure. The opposing view of realism is that the structures are eternally in being, there to be discovered. There is a third view. It denies that human inquiry creates the structure. It affirms that human inquiry discovers it. But human inquiry cannot discover it until the human mind and personality along with the world relative to that mind have been creatively transformed so that the discovery becomes possible. In this sense creativity prior to inquiry must create the structure. Then and then only can human inquiry discover it. Thus the structure need not be eternally in being, but neither does human inquiry create it. Human society, human culture, the human mind and the universe as known to the human mind, must first attain some structure before other structures are possibilities. These other structures may never be discovered but they are in being, there to be discovered, once the mind of man and the culture endowing that mind with all its resources, have reached the level where the discovery becomes a possibility. Beyond what might possibly be discovered, there are no structures to be discovered. When further developments extend what might possibly be discovered, new possibilities come into being, namely, the structures which might possibly be discovered because of the cultural resources now available.

In this sense creativity brings new possibilities into being prior to the actual conduct of inquiry leading to their discovery. This is true if possibility means what is rooted in actual existence. Whitehead invented the notion of a primordial order to contain possibilities not rooted in actual existence. This is conceivable only if we think that possibility is other than the possibilities of actual existence.

When creativity is thus seen to create not only the actuality of the human mind and its culture, but also their possibilities, it can be said that creativity creates *ex nihilo*. It has been demonstrated that, if this is true, creativity cannot be a cosmic person nor a supernatural person. Also, if one wants to find some point of agreement with the existentialists, this view of the matter shows that the divine creativity operating in human life is always at the brink of nothingness, creating possibilities as it goes along. Also creation *ex nihilo* by way of creativity operating in human life and in human history does not involve the self contradiction from which Personalism cannot escape when it tries to show that God is both a person and also creates from nothingness.

Creation from nothingness as here set forth does not entail that there was a point of absolute beginning, when God existed and nothing else did, when God began to create something additional to himself. It is impossible to speak with any intelligibility whatsoever of an absolute beginning and there is no reason to think such an absolute beginning ever was.

After this criticism of Personalism to the effect that a being capable of doing what God is said to do cannot be a person, we shall answer the criticism of those who insist that, nevertheless, the word "God" should not be used if we do not mean to refer to a person, either supernatural or cosmic. Some who insist that God is a person defend the claim by saying that we cannot imagine anything superior to personality. Therefore, since nothing we can imagine is superior to person, God must be a person.

Such a statement is tantamount to saying that my imagination, because it is limited in its capacity, must dictate to God what deity must be. This is precisely what is meant by idolatry. That God should exceed my powers of comprehension is quite to be expected.

To say that God exceeds the powers of our comprehension is not to say that we do not know God. We know empirically the actual, present, dynamic working of creativity in our midst, progressively creating, saving and transforming the personality of man when required conditions are present. Therefore we know God and know him more intimately than any other, because he is so deeply involved in our existence. But to know God thus does not mean that we can construct in our imagination a picture of him or comprehend the depth and fullness of his being.

Still another argument should be noted by which some people try to defend belief in God's personality. It runs like this. "If God is not a person, he cannot love. Therefore God must be a person." Here again is a case of narrow vision. If love means to create, sustain, save from evil and creatively transform toward the greater good, then in that sense God in the form of creativity is the very substance of love. Of course if one means by divine love that God must have that state of consciousness which I experience in myself when I say that I love, then we cannot say that God has any such ambiguous, instable and mixed set of feelings such as I call love in myself. Thank God that God does not love as I do!

Still another argument for belief in God's personality calls for refutation. It rests upon the ground that we use the personal pronoun when we speak of God. But use of the personal pronoun only reveals the inadequacy of our language when we speak of deity. All attempts to speak of the levels of our existence have this difficulty with language. Language has been developed to deal with matters conventional and commonplace. Indeed language is precisely a convention, that is to say, a system of symbols designed to convey conventional meanings common to all the people who use the language. Whenever we reach beyond these limits, our conventional language fails us. So this argument based on the inadequacy of our language is another example of "the human all to human." Since our language is limited and inadequate, we insist that our linguistic usage must dictate to God what deity can be. Surely this cannot be permitted when we approach the greatness of deity.

Another argument, the reverse of the ones we have been considering, has been leveled against the idea of God defended by religious naturalism. It runs like this: What operates in human life to create the human level of existence must itself be the creature of a creativity ontologically prior to human existence. Therefore the creativity operating in human life can only be the creature of the transcendent deity. The transcendent deity is the God beyond God, meaning the God who creates what I call God.

This argument is a fallacy. There is no objection to the claim that the creativity operating in human life to create, sustain, save and transform toward the greater good is continuous with a creativity infinitely transcending human life. I do not myself attempt to defend this claim but if it is true it merely asserts that the creativity in human life is continuous with creativity extending infinitely beyond human life. Furthermore, a creativity not operating in human life can do nothing for man and man can do nothing in relation to it. Therefore no matter how infinitely transcendent creativity may be in its farther reaches, man and God can deal with one another only where man is. The infinite source of this creativity can have religious significance only as it operates in human life. God must come to man, otherwise man cannot reach to

God. But when God comes to man, we have the divine presence here described as creativity. If this creativity operating in human life also extends infinitely beyond human life, everything here said about creativity in human life stands untouched and unchanged.

Sometimes God is depicted in the character of a supernatural person. When this is done the same argument applies which I have just stated. A supernatural person can do nothing with us nor we with him except by way of interchange; and if this interchange is creative, sustaining, saving and transforming, we are back again to the creativity here identified with God. Even if we grant that there is a supernatural person, which I do not, that being in himself can have no religious significance for us; only the creative interchange between that person and ourselves can have religious significance. So here we are, inescapably driven to recognize God in the form of creative interchange.

Next we come to the argument that we cannot pray to God if God is not a person. This is another example of misunderstanding. Prayer or worship is a practice by which we endeavor to renew and deepen our commitment and put ourselves more completely under the control of what saves and transforms creatively. If we do this with a petition deep laid in the organization of personality, then the total self organized around this deep-laid striving of the petition is caught into the creative interchange with other people and into the creative transformation of self in community with them. This does not entail that the other people know anything about the prayer. But when the personality is organized about the prayer, this petition becomes an ingredient in what undergoes creative transformation. In such a case, if the petition does not run counter to the demands of creativity, the outcome of this creative transformation will have a character it would not have if this petition had not been an ingredient in the total process of creativity. In this way prayer can be effective in producing consequences. Therefore it is not true to say that God cannot answer prayer if God operates in the form of creative interchange. No prayer can be effective if it is superficial or if is not profoundly and earnestly sincere. That is to say, as previously stated, the petition must be deep-laid in the organization of the personality. When this is not the case, the petition is not truly an instance of prayer because prayer involves worship and worship involves not merely the utterance of words but the giving of the total self, so far as one is able, in ultimate commitment to the creative and transforming power of God.

It should be noted that all arguments against the claim that God is a person can be gathered together into one statement. The statement is this: God exercises a power different in kind from what any person could ever have.

Last to be examined is a criticism very different from the ones thus far considered. It is made by those who insist that only a transcendent deity can meet the most imperative need, deep laid in human nature. This need, so it is claimed, has always driven great souls to seek salvation by way of religious faith. This most imperative demand is to be delivered from the frustrations, limitations, defeat, guilt, destruction, and death involved in man's finitude. By finitude is meant the structure of personality which man now has along with the structure of society and of the universe. Creativity is said to be entirely immanent, because it operates in human life. Therefore, say these critics, creativity cannot be identified with deity when deity means what men have sought in their outreach beyond the limitations of existence, namely, a transcendent deity or the infinite.

Here again is a misunderstanding. Only by ultimate commitment to creativity can one be delivered from the limitations of this world. Only by way of this commitment can one look upon the structure of the universe, the structure of society and the structure of his own personality, as ephe-

meral, like the passing cloud, because all this undergoes transformation by creativity. With commitment to creativity one
can look beyond all these. With this commitment he does not
depend ultimately upon any known structure of the universe
nor any known structure of human personality or society,
because he is committed to a creativity transforming all of
these. The structures now in existence may destroy his body,
but they cannot destroy his faith and his hope, because he
looks beyond this universe to other universes to be brought
forth by creativity if required conditions are provided for its
effective operation.

The mocking answer to this faith and this hope may be
stated thus: Suppose the human species should be annihilated
by atomic explosions or radioactivity from the cobalt bomb
or by biological destroyers and poison gases? What then becomes of your fine hope and your fine faith? The answer to
that comment is very simple. No religion with any realism in
it has ever said that God would save unless men meet certain
required conditions. So here, men must meet the required
conditions. This is man's responsibility. If God's salvation
came by way of coercion, without any responsibility exercised by man, it would be a self contradiction to call it salvation because it would provide safety without that creative
transformation of man which alone can make life worth
living.

The gigantic increase in man's power makes it possible
for him to provide the conditions required for creativity as
he never could do before. Also this magnified power to
destroy may force men to assume responsibility for recognizing what actually operates to save when required conditions
are present. Heretofore man's power was sufficiently limited
so that men could adopt whatever form of religion might be
provided by tradition or constructed to satisfy psychological
or personal needs or which might be set forth by ontological
or cosmological speculation. This cannot continue if man is to

be saved. There is a creativity able to save; but the prevailing forms of religion do not direct us to it. Our ideals cannot save us, neither can a supernatural person; neither can the enduring structure of the universe; neither can the infinite ground of being, whatever that expression may mean. Only creative transformations can save us.

The prevailing forms of religion may continue to resist the demands of intelligence and empirical knowledge. They may cling to cherished beliefs or to ontological speculation or to psychological tricks or to the highest ideal. If this continues while the power of man increases, religion will be the betrayer and not science nor technology, because it is the responsibility of religion to point to the way of salvation. If the ever increasing power of man is not used to provide conditions under which creativity can operate more effectively than ever before, religion will be the deceiver turning men away from the savior by directing their ultimate commitment to some alleged being other than this creativity, for it alone can save.

CHAPTER FOUR

PAUL TILLICH ANSWERS

With his massive scholarship, his intellectual power and his many profound insights, Paul Tillich has liberated theology from orthodoxy in a decisive manner. Orthodoxy is the result of religious inquiry in past ages. The problems of that earlier time are not identical with the problems of today. Therefore the solving of those problems, to whatsoever measure they may have been solved and put into the form of orthodoxy, cannot be accepted as the solution of the different problems demanding the service of theology in our time. Thus theology, according to Tillich, cannot be orthodox.

His ontology demands the separation and opposition of existential being and essential being. Essential being is what all existence ought to be. Actual existence is opposed to what it ought to be. Therefore it cannot be said that God exists. If you say that God exists, you are saying that God is not what he ought to be. A "God" who is not what he ought to be is not the deity men seek in faith.

God pictured as a cosmic person or a supernatural person is a religious symbol, says Tillich. In truth there is no such actual being but we think of God in this form because it fits our need. This form of thought, otherwise called a religious symbol, is not descriptively true; but it points beyond itself to what Tillich calls "the God beyond God." By this expression he means to say that man's ultimate concern is with the infinite, the power of being or being itself.

Infinite being cannot be described in any way because it exceeds and engulfs every description. Every description is a limitation and the infinite cannot be limited. When we say that God is a person we are making a false statement *unless* we understand that this representation is not a description or definition or characterization of the infinite. Rather it is the form by which we relate ourselves religiously to what concerns us ultimately. When thus used as a symbol, the affirmation, "God is a person," is neither true nor false. Only descriptive or designative statements can be true or false. People may not know that they are using non-cognitive symbols when they pray to a personal God but the theologian must know it if he is a competent interpreter of the faith. This interpretation of the religious symbol combined with the doctrine that God is unknowable being are the two first steps to an understanding of the answer given by Tillich to the question asked by faith.

Tillich's theology rests upon the following assertions: (1) Man's ultimate concern is the infinite, otherwise called the power of being or being itself. (2) The infinite cannot be distinguished from what it is not because the all-encompassing infinite includes everything which might be allegedly distinguished from it. (3) Consequently the religious life, ultimately concerned with the infinite, must be conducted with non-cognitive symbols. These symbols provide no description of the infinite and therefore convey no knowledge of what God may be.

Non-cognitive religious symbols are the central theme in Tillich's theology. To be effective, these symbols must be embodied in a tradition shaping the minds and emotions so that people will experience the reality of what is symbolized when the symbols are used. In this way, says Tillich, symbols participate in what they represent, meaning that one actually experiences not the symbol itself but what it represents. Also it can be said that every symbol participates in the power of being because everything is an instance of being.

Not only must symbols be embodied in a tradition. They must also be constantly interpreted and reinterpreted to fit the changing conditions of human existence and to meet the religious need as it develops under changing conditions. This is the task of the theologian and the preacher. Doing this is what Tillich calls the method of correlation.

The method of correlation, as this term is used by Tillich, means two things. It means, first, that the interpreter of the symbol finds out and experiences in himself what is most disturbing to the people of his time and place and culture. Is it the sense of guilt? Is it the dread of death? Is it the apparent futility of human existence, called the meaninglessness of life? For modern man, says Tillich, it is not so much guilt or dread of death but the apparent futility of all he does which is most disturbing. Hence religious symbols should be interpreted in a way to help the man of our time overcome this loss of meaning in what he does.

The central religious symbol in Christianity is Christ. Tillich is chiefly concerned to interpret Christ as a religious symbol. He speaks not of Jesus Christ but of Jesus as the Christ. This shift in words is significant. It means that for Tillich the important thing is not the man Jesus as he actually existed. Nobody knows the actuality of the man Jesus. What we know is the picture of the man given to us in the New Testament. The man Jesus was not God in any sense of the word. Tillich is emphatic on this point. He says it is absurd to say that the infinite power of being could exist in the form of a man. The man Jesus is important only because he is the source from which arose the picture set forth in the New Testament. So Tillich speaks not of Jesus and not of Jesus Christ but of Jesus as the Christ, meaning Jesus as pictured in the New Testament.

This picture in the New Testament is called the New Being, meaning that man is there pictured as "accepted" by the power of being and thus enabled to overcome non-being. This means to live with courage and hope, love and meaning, while fully acknowledging all the guilt and failure in one's life and the inevitability of death.

The point is not that the picture of Jesus in the Bible serves as a model for us to imitate. Rather what we see in this picture is not the man Jesus but the power of being in the life of this man. As Tillich says, Jesus is transparent so that we see not the man Jesus but being itself represented in him. The man in all he strives to do comes to nothing; but the very nothingness of his personal achievement is the transparency through which we discern the infinite power of being. The New Being is the ecstatic realization by you and me that we are "grasped by" the power of being even in our failure, guilt, frustration, and death. This New Being, this way of life sustained by the power of being, is revealed to us by the way Jesus is pictured in the Bible.

This seems to be what Tillich means when he writes that man's estrangement is overcome "in principle i.e. in power and in beginning . . . in Jesus as the Christ the eternal unity of God and man has become historical." [4]

These words are very liable to be misunderstood. Nothing eternal can be historical. Tillich recognizes this and insists on it. In what sense, then, can "the eternal unity of God and man . . . become historical reality?" It means that the picture of the eternal unity of man's essence with God, set forth in the New Testament, has become historical reality because the New Testament is historical. It does not mean that man in his actual, concrete existence is united with God or ever can be. The vision of this unity does not mean the vision of something that will ever be achieved in history. Neither does it mean the vision of what will be achieved in Heaven. It is not the vision of any future attainment, because eternity cannot be future any more than past. It simply is not temporal at all.

All this is contrary to the Christian message according to Karl Barth. Barth's reply to Tillich will be studied in the next chapter. On this point of disagreement the present writer agrees with Barth. The disciples in fellowship with Jesus did not find a vision of eternal being. They found in that fellowship a kind of interchange which transformed their lives. Barth calls it the Word of God. It was a transformation of their actual, concrete existing selves; and this transformation they passed on to others by the same kind of interchange they had when in fellowship with Jesus. This stands in contrast to Tillich's interpretation of revelation and salvation.

The best way to appraise Tillich's ontological approach to theology and the Christian faith is to see how he deals with the basic problems involved in human existence. His greatness is his insight into these problems and the way he shows them to be the persistent problems of human life. He himself makes plain that any interpretation of religion can be judged to be better or worse, according to the way it treats these inescapable issues arising in every age and culture and in the life of every man. We shall take these problems discussed by Tillich and compare his ontology with the divine creativity to see how each deals with these fundamental issues. This comparison should show which of these two interpretations is best fitted to meet the demands of human existence. This comparison should show which of the two provides the better answer to the question asked by faith. Is the better answer found in the unknowable power of being or in the divine creativity?

The first of these persistent problems inescapably involved in human life is called by Tillich the estrangement between man's existential being and his essential being. The way Tillich deals with this problem has been stated in previous paragraphs of this chapter.

Over against Tillich's treatment of this problem is the opposing view. In opposition to Tillich it is here claimed that man's essential being is what is created by the divine creativity operating in creative interchange. His existential being is the total resultant when this divine creativity is obstructed by counter processes going on in human life. Since the individual becomes what he is not only by this creativity but also by all the opposing processes, his existential being is estranged from his essential being. His essential being in purity and perfection is what he would be if he was completely under the control of creativity and if no counter process entered in to distort what creative interchange would make of him.

In the fellowship with Jesus creative interchange rose to such dominance over counter processes that men got a sense of what the human being would become if he were completely committed to this creativity. This revelation came not by any vision of the ideal and not by any picture of Jesus but by the actual personal experience of living in a fellowship dominated by this creativity. This experience not only reveals what man ought to be (his essential being): it also exposes the contrast between what he actually is (his existential being) and what he ought to be.

This contrast between man's existential being and his essential being reveals the depth and pervasiveness of sin when sin means man's opposition to the divine creativity. The same event opening the way of salvation also reveals the destructive consequences of man's existential being. Only when one experiences to some measure what life *might* be, can one see the evil of what *is*. This prepares the way for the "forgive-ness of sin" whereby the estrangement between existential being and essential being is overcome "in principle," to use Tillich's phrase.

Forgiveness of sin is a total event divided into two parts. The first part is a consequence of emerging insights brought forth by creative interchange. These insights enable me to attain a better understanding of myself and of others. The consequence is that I become able to recognize and accept my "existential predicament of non-being." This "non-being," to use Tillich's language, is my guilt, my sin, my failure and frustration, my inevitable death, the futility of much striv-ing, all the limitations and perversions entering into my life. This is the first part of what is meant by forgiveness of sin. To use a popular cliché, it is self acceptance. More accurately stated, it is acceptance of the truth about oneself.

The second part of the total event called forgiveness of sin is even more important, although it could not occur without this first part. It is the ability to deliver oneself over into the keeping of the divine creativity operating in the kind of interchange we have described. It is the ability to deliver into the keeping of this divine creativity not only one's virtue but also one's sin and guilt, one's failure and frustration, one's futility and death, in a word, one's total being just as he is.

At this point it is of crucial importance to distinguish two kinds of religious commitment, because only one of these ex-emplifies forgiveness. The other kind does not. The kind of commitment which does not include forgiveness of sin is the kind in which the individual delivers to God his virtue, his ideals, all that is good and noble in himself while withholding, as unworthy of divine acceptance, all the sin and evil in him. In contrast to this, the experience called for-giveness of sin is the commitment in which one gives to the divine creativity all the evil in himself as well as the virtue.

This kind of commitment liberates the individual from

"bondage to cynical despair," from "bondage to dogmatic assurance" and from "bondage to unconcern." We use these expressions employed by Tillich not only to show the depth and precision of his analysis but also to show that we are dealing with the same problem as he, but solving it in a different way. This different way is presented as more effectively constructive and empirically demonstrable.

Another problem inescapably involved in human existence and treated at length by Tillich concerns death and other forms of "non-being." The problem is to learn to accept these without concealment or evasion and yet continue to live with courage, faith, hope, and love. How is this possible? Tillich answers by pointing to the New Being. This is the vision of the eternal unity of man's essential being with the power of being.

There is another way to answer this question. The individual can accept his death, his limitations and frustrations if they help him to attain the ruling purpose of his life more amply than he could do without them. If the ruling purpose of one's life is to commit himself most completely to the divine creativity, these limitations called non-being enable him to do so more fully than he could do without them. If one could drive on under his own power he would never be thrown back on the need and practice of commitment to creative interchange. Without frustration, futility and other limitations, man would not have the unfulfilled potentialities calling for transformation. Thus these limitations are indispensable to the destiny distinguishing him from every other animal.

In this context death calls for special treatment. With commitment to creativity death can be accepted as a necessary condition for the most complete attainment of the ruling purpose of one's life. Unless individuals in one generation die, the innumerable individuals in subsequent generations will not have space and opportunity to develop and make their contribution to the growth of cultural resources required for the progressive creation of man. Unless the power of individuals in one generation is limited, other individuals beginning with infancy and childhood cannot develop freely and fully. The unlimited power of the first generation would be too dominant and domineering.

My own death and limitation of my own power I cannot accept as good merely because other individuals are benefited thereby. But if I give myself to the divine creativity sufficiently to attain the great good which it can do for me, I shall in that very act of commitment find all things good which promote the work of this creativity because I have identified myself with it so that what is good for it is good for me. When this occurs, I can accept my own death and my limitation of power when these are seen to be the necessary conditions for the effective operation of this creativity throughout human history.

Innumerable diverse individuals must make unique contributions generation after generation to the accumulating cultural resources through the ages if man is to undergo creative transformation by increase in the five dimensions of personality described in previous chapters. This requires that each individual die after making his contribution so that others can make theirs. Thus for him whose ultimate commitment is rightly directed, death has its own proper place and value.

In so far as one's death and other limitations of power are the necessary conditions for the most effective work of this divine creativity, the individual committed to the living God who works throughout history in this way will accept as good his own death and other limitations which contribute to the progressive creation of man.

It is not here suggested that there is necessarily a progressive accumulation of resources for human living so that ever higher individual attainment becomes possible. Yet there has been a great accumulation of these resources since the first ape-man began to use the meager beginning of linguistic signs. The monstrous evils of history are not denied nor obscured in the claim here made for the divine creativity. The evil does not reduce in any way the good. The good stands in its own right, untarnished and undiminished by the evil. True, every concrete form of existence contains ambiguously a mixture of good and evil. But the good is there along with the evil. Presence of evil does not diminish value of the good. The good is what is produced by, and what promotes, the divine creativity throughout human history.

He who is ultimately committed to the divine creativity can say: All the good produced throughout human history by divine creativity is my good. No matter how tiny my contribution, no matter how brief my days and foolish my ways, no matter how near my death, all this work of divine creativity throughout human history is what gives to my life its meaning, its purpose and its magnitude of value. No one can say this sincerely unless in truth he has made the divine creativity in history the ruling purpose and supreme devotion of his life and has made the kind of commitment previously described as forgiveness of sin. Then and only then he can say in all truth and in the midst of "weakness, necessities, persecutions, and distresses" that he is "more than conqueror through Christ" when Christ means this divine creativity working throughout the length and breadth of human history.

This is the answer to the question: How live with courage, faith, hope and love while fully acknowledging all the evils of life? These evils are called by Tillich the "destructive consequences of existential being." This statement is here accepted as profoundly true, provided that existential being is defined as resistance to the divine creativity. But this source of courage must be found as an actuality, not as the power of being beyond existence and essence. No matter what vision in the form of New Being one may have of this non-actual being, it cannot do for man what the actuality of the divine creativity can do. Neither can man do for it, what man can do for this creativity. What man can do for this creativity gives the maximum meaning to his existence.

This sense of the great good of the divine creativity through history may be dim and vague to the mind of the individual, but it can be more or less vivid, more or less powerful in its motivation for living. Like any other sustaining purpose which may motivate human life, it can be cultivated by symbol and ritual in public ceremony and private practice. If this commitment were widely practiced so that thousands and millions celebrated it together, and if this continued through several generations so that the entire life of the individual was caught into its driving power, the so-called limitations of finitude would be accepted not as obstructions and frustrations but as contributory to the ruling purpose of life. Death in its proper place and time would be a good and not an evil. Life would never be meaningless no matter how small the achievement of the individual. The decline of one civilization and the rising dominance of another would not be black catastrophe.

By no means would life lived in this way find all things to be good. Far from it. By this commitment monstrous evils are exposed which can be perceived only when the standard for judging good and evil is the divine creativity. The divine creativity might itself be overcome and annihilated. But all this evil cannot diminish the blessedness and the beauty of the good. In the form of the divine creativity the good of life shines forth, extending immeasurably beyond the life of the individual, unlimited by his personal successes and failures, endowing his devotion and his striving with a greatness reaching throughout the entire expanse of human history.

We human beings are carriers of the divine creativity and on that account have a responsibility which cannot be repudiated. No speculation about what divine power might be or do after human life is destroyed, can deliver us from this responsibility. To be the carrier of this divine creativity is the glory of human existence. This glory may pass away. The tragedy of this passing is in no way relieved by speculations about the divine creativity passing on to some form of life elsewhere in the universe or developing out of some lower form of existence. These speculations merely divert attention and devotion from our responsibility as carriers of the divine creativity in human history amid the storms of temporal existence. Here is where the vocation and the tragedy must be lived and nowhere else.

Temporality in the sense of the passing of all things dear is one of the limitations of man which the individual can learn to accept because of its contribution to the divine creativity. When properly interpreted in the form of symbol and art, what has passed away can make its enduring contribution to the scope and depth of meaning which our language can bear, understanding by language not only that of common usage but likewise all forms of art. So, if the work of this creativity is what we live for, and if the good we prize in life is what it does, our temporality can be accepted as a blessing even though it has its pang.

In the same way commitment to divine creativity enables a man to accept his suffering and loneliness, his insecurity and uncertainty. These also are necessary conditions for the attainment of the greater good by way of divine creativity. The greater good is brought forth by unpredictable innovations expanding the range of what man can appreciate as good and distinguish as evil. These innovations and transformations produce in us the sense of uncertainty and insecurity, or loneliness and suffering. While these are negative values in one dimension, in another dimension, namely, that of the divine creativity, they have positive value.

It is impossible to measure the good and evil of life by adding the good and subtracting the evil in all the different dimensions, as though these values all belonged to the same dimension. What is negative in one dimension can be positive when appraised relative to another. It makes all the difference which dimension is the one where the individual seeks his treasure. If one is quite completely committed to one dimension, his life will be good or evil depending on the values in this dimension, no matter what the values may be in other dimensions. So it is when one commits himself to the values to be found in the dimension of the divine creativity. Death and limited power, temporality and failure of particular undertakings, insecurity and uncertainty, suffering and loneliness, are evils in some dimensions. But in the dimension of divine creativity they can take on positive value for the individual if he is ultimately committed to this creativity. In this dimension and by commitment to divine creativity, one can overcome what Tillich calls non-being far more effectively than is possible by way of what he calls the New Being.

A further problem is treated by Tillich, and he rightly says it is necessarily involved in human existence. It is that of uniting "dynamics and form." Here again we highly esteem his analysis of the problem but cannot accept his proposed solution of it.

Dynamics refers to any kind of process whatsoever which produces consequences. Form is any distinguishable product brought forth by the process. "Dynamics" is identical in meaning with the word "process." At least this is true when the word "process" is used as we are using it here. "Form" is identical in meaning with the word "structure."

With this understanding of the words, the problem under consideration has two sides to it. (1) How can the process of dynamics be so directed and regulated that it will produce forms of high value? (2) How can forms be of high intrinsic value and also serve to direct and regulate the process so that it will continue to produce forms of high value?

What we have said about the divine creativity should make it plain that this problem also finds its solution when one commits himself to God understood as this process. The dynamics producing forms of great value are the interchanges creating appreciative understanding of one another on the part of individuals. The forms created by this process are the forms of love and fellowship, beauty, justice and power. Above all, this interchange creates the form of noble personality.

When the individual and the fellowship of individuals give first priority to the demands of creative interchange, the forms created by this interchange feed back into the creativity to magnify its power. This is precisely what is meant by solving the problem of dynamics and form. So here again we see that commitment to the process of creative interchange solves the problem of dynamics and form which Tillich rightly says is one of the persistent problems of human existence but which his ontology does not solve so well as it is solved by the divine creativity actually operating in human life.

Another problem inextricably involved in human living and exposed by Tillich's analysis pertains to freedom and destiny. The problem is to understand how these two are related and how life can be conducted so that one of them does not disrupt the other. Here again we accept with admiration Tillich's statement of the problem.

According to Tillich freedom is decision controlled and directed by the unifying center of the structure which is the individual's own self. Destiny is the control exercised by this very structure which is the individual with his biological and cultural heritage and the total situation making him what he is. This structure determines the form and limit of the possibilities from which the individual can choose without being self destructive and without impairing his freedom. If the individual chooses what is excluded by this structure, he will destroy the very structure which gives him his freedom. The chapter on freedom will explain the way creative interchange creates freedom within the structure of individuality. (Chapter Eight)

Tillich says that the power of being is the "depth of reason." But this "depth of reason" is not reason at all according to what Tillich himself says about reason. Reason, he rightly says, is either some specifiable structure or some statement which correctly specifies it. Reason in neither of these two senses can be attributed to the power of being. The latter can be called the depth of reason only in the sense that reason, like folly, stupor, insanity and anything else you wish to mention, is an instance of being. The power of being includes and transcends all of these. Consequently, when one says that power of being is the depth of reason, the statement can only mean that reason is an instance of being. But the opposite of reason is just as truly an instance of being.

Tillich goes on to say that power of being has time in its depth. Here again we have the same kind of tautology or else a contradiction of what Tillich has said about power of being. Time is a temporal sequence. Power of being cannot be identified with temporal sequence. Yet temporal sequence is an instance of being along with its opposite. So also are microbes and green cheese. If Tillich means to say that time is in the depth of being but not in the form of temporal sequence, he is saying that time is not time. So here again we are forced to choose between tautology and self contradiction.

The power of being has space in its depth, says Tillich. Space in the depth of being is either a form of spatial expanse or it is not. If not in the form of spatial expanse, it is not space. If it is, he contradicts what he says about power of being. The power of being cannot be a spatial expanse. If he merely means to say that space is an instance of being, we again have the sterile tautology.

Tillich has much more of this sort to say about the power of being. He says that it has cause in its depth and also substance. The criticism we have just made applies to all these statements. Being is the most comprehensive term in human use and so applies to everything. If this is all that Tillich means to say with all these claims for the power of being, his affirmations have no special significance for religious living.

The power of being has in it the divine life of creativity, says Tillich. But this "creativity" in the power of being is not a temporal process bringing something new into existence. It cannot be because power of being, according to Tillich's own teaching, cannot be an occurrence in the temporal sequence of events. Therefore this alleged creativity in the power of being is not creativity at all unless Tillich merely means to say that creativity, like everything else, is an instance of being.

The power of being is Spirit, says Tillich. He explains that Spirit refers to the divine life of meaning. But this divine life of meaning in the power of being is not a temporal development progressively attaining anticipated goals. A "life of meaning" which does not assume this form is not a life of meaning.

The power of being is love, says Tillich. Tillich himself defines love as a uniting of what has been separated. A uniting of what has been separated is an instance of being, but so is the opposite.

The power of being is freedom, says Tillich. But this freedom is not what Tillich himself says freedom must be. Freedom, he says, is decision and action under the control of the organizing center of a structured individual. Power of being is not a structured individual.

Final revelation of God, according to Tillich, is distinguished by its capacity to overcome the oppositions between autonomy and heteronomy in the exercise of reason. Autonomy of reason is its exercise for its own sake and not to serve an ultimate commitment beyond itself. Its heteronomy is its exercise under the control of some authority imposed by men. This humanly constructed authority may be the business corporation, the advertiser, the state, the church. Most commonly in the field of religion the heteronomy of reason is displayed when it is exercised to defend the sanctity of a religious tradition.

In contrast both to autonomy and heteronomy is the theonomy of reason. Theonomy overcomes the opposition between autonomy and heteronomy. When reason is exercised under the control of the divine creativity and in its service, theonomy of reason is attained. Here again a basic problem involved in human existence is better mastered by way of the divine creativity than by Tillich's ontology.

A further feature distinguishing final revelation, according to Tillich, is that it overcomes the conflict between absolutism and relativism. This conflict arises when anything set up as the absolute standard for judging better and worse and right and wrong prevents recognition and just appreciation of all the innumerable forms of good and evil which are relative in the sense of changing their character in relation to different individuals, cultures, situations and periods of time. The absolute standard cannot change. It is the same for every person in every time and place, in every culture and age.

How can this claim for the absolute standard be reconciled with the claim that what is good for one person is not good for another, and what is right or wrong in one culture is not in another? These diverse demands changing from person to person, from culture to culture and from age to age, are the relative values. Each relative value is valid in its own time and place and should not be suppressed or denied by the absolute standard. How can the absolute and the relative be reconciled so that the absolute shall stand unchanged while providing for the thronging diversity of relative values?

Any revelation accepted as final must resolve this conflict in such a way that the one supreme good, called absolute, is recognized and served above all, in every time and place, while at the same time permitting the relative values to be served and sought.

This reconciliation of the absolute and the relative is accomplished in Jesus as the Christ when this revelation is interpreted to be creative interchange risen to dominance over counter processes. In revelation thus interpreted the absolute is that kind of interchange which (1) creates appreciative understanding of the diverse values in each unique individual, culture and situation and (2) enables each to integrate into his own individuality the appreciations of good and the distinctions of evil achieved through mutual criticism and reconstruction occurring in this interchange. When the absolute takes this form it magnifies all the relative values. Yet the absolute standard continues unchanged and supreme in its authority over relative values.

Still another feature distinguishing final revelation, according to Tillich, is the reconciliation of formalism and emotionalism. In religion, in art, in inter-personal relations and in the practical conduct of affairs, strong emotion tends to cast off the discipline of control prescribed by proper form. On the other hand, conduct rigorously controlled by observing proper form tends to become cold and formal. The classical example of this opposition between form and emotionalism is found in the writings of St. Paul. He condemns formalism in the pharasaic striving to obey the law. He also condemns the emotionalism in the churches addicted to "speaking with tongues." The two are united and reconciled in the law of love in Christ. So says Tillich.

But the "law of love in Christ" conceals the problem instead of solving it, when this verbal formula is allowed to stand without further interpretation. There can be no law of love when that means to love in obedience to a command. But there can be a law of love when that means to accept as absolute the law that one strive in every situation to provide conditions most favorable for appreciative understanding and integration of diverse values by mutual criticism and reconstruction between one's own system of values and that of others. When this occurs we have all the emotion which profound appreciation of values can arouse but this emotion occurs in those forms required for fullest and widest understanding of self and others and of the situation in which this kind of interchange occurs.

The kind of interchange reconciling formalism and emotionalism in the way just described is the revelation of God in Christ when the revelation is interpreted in terms of the divine creativity of interchange.

The conflict between subjectivity and objectivity must be overcome by final revelation, says Tillich. This is the conflict between the self and world when "world" refers to what the individual can recognize as the established order with all individuals and things related to one another by this order. When the individual subordinates the demands of his own self to something in the world, whether it be the state or the church or the technology of an industrial society or a husband or wife or family or occupation, the self is dwarfed. It becomes a "cog" in the mechanism. On the other hand, when any of these are subordinated to the demands of the self, the demands of the world are denied and the self becomes arrogant, domineering and unjust.

This conflict between subjectivity and objectivity cannot be rightly corrected by compromise when this means that each of the opposing demands is reduced to a level where they balance one another in opposition. This will not do because each of these two demands should be satisfied to the maximum, not reduced to a minimum.

This maximum satisfaction of both demands without compromise or conflict is revealed in Jesus as the Christ when this revelation is interpreted to be the kind of interchange which creates both self and world progressively and reciprocally, when required conditions are present. Thus self and world are united in the source creating them both. When ultimate commitment is given not to the world as object nor to the self as subject, but to the creativity transforming both of them, the conflict is overcome. The conflict arises when the self tries to use the world or some part of it to serve the self; or some part of the world (state, church, technology or something else) tries to use the self for its own ends. In either case we have the conflict between subjectivity and objectivity. But when both self and world are subordinated to the demands of creative interchange, both are progressively created in a way to serve one another.

Thus we see again that revelation in Jesus as the Christ meets the requirements of final revelation provided that Tillich's ontology is disregarded, and creative interchange is put in its place.

Final revelation is manifestation of the Holy, says Tillich. The Holy he defines (Vol. II, p. 113) as the annihilating power of the divine presence called the *tremendum*, and its elevating power, called the *fascinosum*.

When creativity rises to that high level of dominance which is the revelation in Christ, a shattering experience of being reconstructed occurs. The organization of personality undergoes a change so radical that what has been known and appreciated heretofore fades into nothingness. But this is transitional to a transformed self and a transformed world more comprehensive of goods appreciated and evils distinguished. The shattering experience of being reconstructed is the *tremendum* of annihilating power. The emergence of a transformed self and a transformed world is the *fascinosum*

INTELLECTUAL FOUNDATION OF FAITH

of elevating power. The classic example of this is the experience of Saul the Pharisee on the road to Damascus when
he was transformed into Paul the Saint.

Thus final revelation has the distinguishing characteristic
of the Holy, when God is identified with the creativity in
interchange, but not if we go along with Tillich in identify-
ing God with being itself. Tillich admits that being itself cannot be experienced as holy except in the form of a symbol;
and no symbol can give us any knowledge of the infinitive
power of being. Furthermore, being itself, unless identified
with creativity, is not an actual operating power, therefore
cannot be both "annihilating" and "elevating."

The purpose of this criticism of Tillich's theology has
been to demonstrate that the problems involved in human
existence, which must be continuously treated to sustain life
at the level distinctively human, can be better mastered by
commitment to the divine creativity than by Tillich's ontology. Why, then, does Tillich adopt the ontology of being
itself and reject that of creativity in seeking an answer to the
question of faith?

Tillich himself answers that question quite plainly. He
asserts that the ultimate religious question is this: How can
man conquer non-being, when "non-being" refers to all the
limitation, frustration and destruction encountered in human
existence? By "overcome" he does not mean eliminate. He
means to be able to accept with courage, faith, hope and
love. This is the basic religious problem to solve, as seen by
Tillich. When this is understood to be the question, the only
answer is the power of being itself, says Tillich. The divine
creativity set forth in this writing as the living God cannot
answer this question, Tillich seems to think, because it can
be opposed by counter processes. Whatever can be opposed
can conceivably be overcome. Everything in existence is subject to this contingency. It can disappear entirely, giving

place to something else entirely opposed to it. Therefore nothing in existence can answer the religious question according to Tillich's reasoning.

This view of the religious problem leads Tillich to reject everything in existence, even the existence of God, and turn to what lies beyond existence and beyond every limited form of possibility. This he calls the power of being or being itself. This solves his problem because being can never be destroyed.

My reply to all this can be stated unequivocally. It is true that being itself can never be destroyed because everything whatsoever is an instance of being. No matter what is destroyed, whatever remains is still a form of being. All life might be destroyed and all the stars and planets, leaving only a dim kind of radiation. That radiation would still be an instance of being. Everything conceivable might be destroyed; leaving what we cannot conceive. What we cannot conceive would still be an instance of being. The slow and ghastly torture of the human race to the point of extinction would still manifest the power of being.

This is the only kind of indestructibility which being itself or the power of being can provide. The form of words used by Tillich seems to give assurance of beneficent eternity. But the eternity of being itself is nothing more than the certainty that something will be when all life and virtue have ceased. This is no adequate answer to the question asked by faith.

It is true that we live in the midst of danger and destruction. Yet the greatest good is available to each. It is found in commitment to the divine creativity. He who identifies himself with this source of all human good, experiences in his own person the good which it creates, precisely because he has identified himself with it. All the good brought forth by this creativity in ages past and in ages yet to come is the personal good of him whose life is given to the service of this divine presence.

This is not mysticism. In limited range it is a very common experience. Many a parent or lover has identified himself with the beloved so that the good and evil of the other, his suffering and his joy, become the same for the parent or the lover. The good and evil of a man's life is determined by that to which he is most completely committed. Hence he who commits himself most completely to the divine creativity brings into his own life all the good which this divine being has done, is doing and will do throughout human history.

To say that we should not give ourselves in ultimate commitment to this creativity because it might not go on forever, or might never prevail over counter processes, is like saying one should never love with the whole heart because love can fail; or one should never undertake anything good and noble because his efforts might come to nothing; or one should never seek to solve a difficult problem because error can always occur. He who cowers through life like that is unfit for human existence because he does not make the ultimate commitment.

In wide ranges of human life the divine creativity is beaten down and overlaid with hate, fear, envy, pride, greed, malice, stupor, misery, and vicious perversity. But it continues at some level and to some degree wherever human life continues. It rises anew with every newborn infant and for a time there is a struggle between two opposing forces. On the one hand is the divine creativity whereby the child learns to understand and appreciate the thoughts and feelings of associates and communicate this understanding in the form of language and other signs. Opposed to this, is the wrong treatment of the child by parents and others, causing fear, hate, envy and other counter processes. As these develop in the child they beat down and overlay the divine creativity in the life of the growing individual. The cynic looks at this tragic development and says it is ridiculous to commit yourself to the divine creativity. The cynic misses the greatest good which life can offer because he never commits himself to it.

The existentialists are right in saying that existence in its depth and totality is not rational and not moral. Obscurity and irrationality underlie the order in the world and in our lives. Surging destructiveness breaks forth at times to overwhelm the order. But in the midst of all this, the divine creativity generates insights leading to rational and moral order, to beauty and love, to community and culture. It calls for the commitment men have given to God. What in truth requires that kind of commitment is in truth the living God.

Names are not important except to indicate the right attitude toward what is named. The name of God indicates that what bears this name calls for the place of supreme control in our lives and, when given this place, will save from destructive consequences in whatsoever measure that is possible. The divine creativity portrayed in this writing has this character. Therefore the name of God is the name indicating its true significance. Without this name its true significance is likely to be lost.

Men have thought of God in many different forms. In respect to these mental pictures we must choose between two courses. One is to cling to the form which happens to be given in our tradition. The other is to seek to know what truly has the power to save when accepted as supreme, no matter how different the form of it may be from the mental picture in the minds of men. We must choose between the mental picture and the actual creativity transforming and saving when required actual conditions are present. The old sad story is that men cling to the mental picture and ignore the actual creativity until, like a buffalo herd plunging to death over a cliff, they cannot be saved. They believe what the herd believes and not what the evidence indicates.

Where shall we seek to find the divine presence? Shall we seek in the realm of the ideal? Yes, says John Dewey. Shall we seek for a cosmic person? Yes, says the religious personalist speaking through Brightman, and Bertocci. Shall we seek the infinite being, the God beyond God? Yes, says Paul Tillich. Shall we seek God in the form of a spoken Word, giving to this Word the interpretation of Karl Barth? Yes, says Karl Barth. Over against these alternatives is the one here defended. God is found in the divine creativity empirically transforming man as he cannot transform himself, thereby expanding the range of what he can know and control, can appreciate as good and distinguish as evil, can understand evaluatively in the unique individuality of his fellow men and himself.

Philosophers generally seek either ideal perfection or infinite being or cosmic wholeness when they engage in religious inquiry. But the mass of humanity cry for salvation. On this point the common man is wiser than the philosopher because ideal perfection and infinite being and cosmic wholeness can mean nothing to the individual until he is creatively transformed after the manner just described. More important still, ideal perfection, infinite being and cosmic wholeness must be progressively apprehended by creative transformation of man and society through the sequence of generations continuing through history. Therefore these philosophers should recognize that their ultimate commitment should be given to the divine creativity as it operates in each individual, in society and history, when required conditions are present. When the philosopher refuses to commit himself above all else to this creativity, he is claiming that he has no need for any further creative transformation. Many a philosopher seems to have made this claim, but every other philosopher disagrees with him on this point.

Recognizing the ontological priority of divine creativity over human creativity is of utmost practical importance. This priority means that men must use their power of creativity to provide the conditions most favorable for divine creativity to generate the insight which can widen and deepen appreciative understanding between diverse individuals and groups. When this is not done, the more power men acquire, the more self-destructive they become. This follows inevitably because, when appreciative understanding is not widened and deepened along with the increase of power, the power of each is exercised to frustrate, exploit and destroy the ordered life of others. Then death and chaos break forth.

The great contribution which Tillich has made to religious inquiry I here repeat. He has broken free of the cramping traditionalism and empty forms which commonly confine and mislead religious inquiry. At the same time he has sought earnestly to find whatever truth can be discovered by devoted study of the religious tradition. His freedom, his search and his discoveries we applaud. The criticism here made of him applies to the teaching that man's ultimate concern is directed to the power of being. Not power of being but divine creativity actually operative in human existence is the ultimate concern of man. In religion this cannot be mere concern; it must be ultimate commitment.

CHAPTER FIVE

KARL BARTH ANSWERS

The answer given by Karl Barth to the question asked by faith contradicts the answer of Paul Tillich on every major point. According to Barth God is a definite, distinguishable being whereas for Tillich God is the power of being without distinguishable character. Barth teaches that we cannot know God by drawing on the resources of philosophy, psychology, art and the social sciences because God must take the initiative and make himself known. Tillich draws upon all the resources just mentioned to give meaning to religious symbols. For Tillich these serve to guide the conduct of religious living in place of any descriptive knowledge of God.

Barth denies that we can reason from the contingency of all existence to the certain conclusion that God is the necessary being underlying and sustaining these contingent forms of existence. This line of reasoning, from contingent existence to necessary being, leads Tillich to his ontology with the doctrine that the God beyond God is being itself. Barth says that God cannot be identified with our ideals of love, freedom, justice, and fatherhood, even when these are imaginatively projected to the utmost perfection because ideals are constructions of the human mind whereas God is an actuality qualitatively different and superior to these. For Tillich the ideals of love, freedom, justice, and the like are the symbols by which we relate ourselves to God.

Barth insists that God became a man living at that one place in that time and in the concrete situation and that this is literally true without any symbolism or qualification mixed into it. Tillich says it is absurd to claim that being itself could ever assume the form of a man although the man Jesus as pictured in the Bible has a transparency through which we can discern the power of being. Barth explicitly repudiates the picture, saying that it must be the man himself as he actually lived who is identical with God.

Barth teaches that heaven is a locality with its own time and space; and life after death in heaven will be a bodily existence. Tillich denies that individuals will continue to exist in bodily form after death. These statements by Barth and Tillich made in opposition to one another might be continued.

Barth writes: "God exists, lives and acts and makes himself known." [5] Men cannot know God by speculative reason, says Barth. But we can have definite knowledge of God when God makes himself known by His "Word" spoken in Jesus Christ and in the apostles and prophets. This knowledge of God is only attainable when there is "illumination of the reason." It is knowledge received from God given to those who have been elected by divine grace to receive it. Others cannot have this knowledge from God because the human mind is incapable of believing it until God gives the individual the "freedom to believe."

This knowledge from God is "living knowledge," otherwise called wisdom. "Wisdom is the knowledge by which we may actually and practically live; it is empiricism and it is the theory which dominates our life, which is really a light upon our path." (p. 25)

The truth of Jesus Christ and the knowledge of God derived from exegesis of the Bible is not, according to Barth, a system of propositions discovered by study of the Bible and accepted as true statements. Rather this truth must be constantly recovered and kept alive by interchange within the church. Thus the Word of God, for Barth, is not merely printed words in the Bible. Words in the Bible are not the Word of God unless they create a community and this community, which is the church, must be constantly criticized, recovered, and renewed by interchange among its members. This kind of communication going on in the church is the way the living knowledge of God in Christ is kept alive. This is the teaching of Barth and it sounds very much like creative interchange.

Yet Barth would not accept the divine creativity operating in creative interchange as identical with the Word of God. Much of what he says about the Word of God can be said about this creativity. But much else said by Barth cannot be reconciled with it.

For Barth the intellectual foundation of faith is the Word of God; and the Word of God is entirely "inaccessible and inconceivable" to the natural powers of the human mind. No one, no matter how great his intellectual powers, can ever understand aright the Word of God unless God himself has selected that person as one to whom "grace" is given whereby he becomes "free" to believe the Word of God in spite of contrary evidence.

> . . . the believer in God's Word may hold on to this Word in everything in spite of all that contradicts it. Men in the Bible did not come to faith by reason of any kind of proofs, but one day they were so placed that they might believe and then had to believe in spite of everything.

God is hidden from us outside His Word. But He is manifest to us in Jesus Christ. If we look past Him, we must not be surprised if we fail to find God and experience errors and disillusionment . . . we must believe in spite of God's hiddenness . . . We do not believe out of personal reason and power.[6]

Barth gives praise that he is one of the elect chosen by God to receive the grace whereby a man has the freedom to believe what cannot be supported by evidence outside the Bible and cannot even be supported by any study of the words of the Bible unless one has the gift from God to get the truth accessible only to those who have been elected. Without this special grace the great intellects of the world cannot dispute the teachings of Barth because this grace and this only enables one to know what Barth knows.

These claims and many others like them to be found in the writings of Barth seem to say that rational coherence and other forms of evidence do not apply to the knowledge of God. This knowledge must be given to us and we must accept it no matter how lacking the evidence and no matter how contradictory the affirmations. "The greatest hindrance to faith is again and again just the pride and anxiety of our human hearts. We would rather not live by grace. Something within us energetically rebels against it." (p. 20)

When we demand rational coherence and supporting evidence before we can accept the Word of God as taught by Barth, we do thereby show pride. Even when we demand rational coherence and supporting evidence in our interpretation of the Bible and on that account cannot find in the Bible what Barth finds, we show that we have not received grace from God giving us the freedom to believe. Again it is our pride getting in the way and rejecting God's grace. Failing to find the truth found by Barth and other recipients of

God's grace, we are filled with anxiety. So, writes Barth: "This swing to and fro between pride and anxiety is man's life. Faith bursts through them both." (p. 20)

Barth summarizes his view of the intellectual foundation of faith in the following words:

> If we summarise all that opposes the acceptance of God's Word as the power of contradiction, one has an inkling of what Scripture means by the devil. "Has God really said . . . ?" Is God's Word true? If one believes, one will snap his finger at the devil. (p. 20)

The devil to which Barth refers in this quotation is the principle of non-contradiction. It cannot be applied to God's Word. We snap our fingers at it when it seems to render unbelievable what we have the freedom to believe by God's grace. Barth does indeed admit that we carry "this treasure in earthen vessels," meaning that our interpretation and understanding of the truth given of God is subject to error. But this presents a dilemma for him which he does not seem to recognize. Either God's grace delivers him from error or it does not. If it does, then he can never be in error when he proclaims the truth of God. If it does not save him from error, then all he says about the grace of God enabling one to know what the natural powers of human reason cannot know falls to the ground.

In dispute with Barth one cannot appeal to the Bible as authority because no human mind can find the truth of God's Word in the Bible unless he has received the grace from God given to Barth. This leaves Barth and those who agree with him the sole arbiters of the truth. Paul Tillich is not one who has received this grace of God, because Barth writes in his introduction to *Dogmatics in Outline* that Tillich's procedure in his *Systematic Theology* is entirely mistaken. Barth throughout his *Dogmatics in Outline* puts into italics terms used by Tillich to show that the latter is in error on the major points of theology.

On one major point Karl Barth is right. He seeks foundations for religious faith which cannot be shaken nor in any wise disturbed by doubt, error, defeat, disaster, despair and death. Such a faith one must have if it is to carry a man through the storms of human existence as the great religious personalities of history have lived. A faith without such foundations does not display the distinctive character of high religion. Barth is right and all who disagree with him are wrong if they fail to recognize that religious faith must have a basis whereby it can sustain a man through every doubt and every despair. Many who proclaim a faith in opposition to Barth have not established such a base on which to stand when all the world falls to pieces around them. In so far as Karl Barth sees that religious faith must have this character, while they who oppose him do not see it, he is right and they are wrong.

The criticism here made of Barth is not directed to his striving to have a faith beyond the reach of all the assaults of fortune. Rather the criticism is directed to the way he endeavors to establish it. He tries to render faith immune to doubt by rejecting the demands of natural human reason.

There is another way to find foundations of faith beyond the reach of doubt and despair. This other way must here be set forth if our criticism is to be constructive as well as destructive. The problem is to establish a foundation for faith beyond the reach of doubt while accepting all the demands of human reason and putting no limit upon doubt and criticism. A foundation of faith depending upon protective devices to ward off rational doubt and critical inquiry, such as Barth proposes, cannot stand. There is another way and this we shall explain.

First of all the fallibility of the human mind must be

admitted and no alleged grace of God can save it from error, no matter what pronouncement is made. The only assertion with which to begin is the claim that we experience a difference between better and worse. One can doubt that and argue over it, but if you touch him with a red hot iron his behavior belies all his arguments. Anything can be disputed and argued so long as one keeps within the arena of the purely academic, but in actual life no one doubts the reality of a distinction between better and worse. Or, one can put the matter in another way. The concern of religious faith arises only when we recognize the distinction of better and worse. If anyone does not admit this distinction, he is not within the field of religious concern. Religious faith is essentially a question about better and worse. If there be a human being who does not ask what is better and what is worse, such a one is outside the universe of discourse where the religious question is asked. Furthermore, we are asking how faith can stand unshaken by disaster, doubt, and despair. One who never experiences the difference between better and worse cannot experience disaster, doubt and despair and so could not be involved in this discussion.

Perhaps the best way to expose the foundation of faith beyond the reach of doubt and despair is to present faith in the form of a confession after the following manner.

Suppose a man makes his confession of faith in words like these: I am committed to what I believe can bring human life to the best it can ever attain, when required conditions are met. I am not committed to my belief. My belief is merely the means by which I give my life's devotion to what transforms life toward the greater good. If it be necessary I shall die in this service under the guidance of this belief, not because I can be sure that my belief is true, but because I have no other way of giving myself to what is supremely important for all human living. If my belief should be in error, if all my efforts should be contrary to what I want to serve above all else, then I can only hope that my work will be destroyed or come to nothing. If it be true that I am working against what I want most to promote, my faith still stands because my intention is to serve what I am unintentionally opposing.

This confession is not merely the expression of the futility of good intentions. My belief has not been lightly taken. It is the result of devoted searching and thinking, always in readiness to correct any error when discovered. When I confess that I might be in error, I am only admitting the fallibility of the human mind. I am not saying that I doubt what I believe. I am only admitting the possibility of error which honesty demands. This does not prevent me from gathering up all the resources of my life into a single package and delivering it to this devotion and this service. Error is not fatal provided that it keeps open the way for correction. Perhaps all the great truths have been discovered in consequence of correcting initial error. In many cases error cannot be discovered until someone pursues it to the end and thereby exposes the disastrous consequences. If my service to God can be nothing more than to expose the error of my belief, then this is the service I offer because it is the best I can do.

If all my life must be given to exposing an error, if all I do must in the end be wiped out as obstructive to the good I serve, then this is my devotion. It is living and dying in pursuit of an illusion to the end that others may see that it is an illusion. This is not what I believe I am doing. I am very confident, after seeking in every way to be purged of error, that I am in the right. But the ultimate foundation of my faith can stand through every doubt, every failure, even through every defeat. It can stand unshaken through all of this because it does not rest on the assumption that God has given me grace to know the truth beyond the natural powers of the human mind. I can accept error. I need not protect my belief against the liability to error precisely because the foundation of my faith is not a part of the structure of belief built upon it. The structure of belief can be wiped away and the foundation still stands because the foundation is this: Whatever in truth can bring life to the best attainable is what I serve, even though my beliefs about it are mistaken and even though all I do even to the point of sacrificing my life is unintentionally obstructive to it.

A life lived in this way would be tragic, to be sure. But tragedy is not the ultimate evil. Faith can stand unshaken by tragedy. He who has this foundation of faith can accept tragedy into his faith after this manner. He who cannot admit this possible tragedy, he who must try to protect against it by claiming special grace from God to give him cognitive capacity beyond the natural powers of human reason, cannot survive disillusion. Such a one is open to an ultimate doubt and an ultimate despair from which there is no recovery. But the basis of faith here confessed always has a source of recovery beyond the reach of every doubt, every error, defeat, disaster, despair, and final death.

He who confesses his faith on the basis here exposed will say: This is my life and if it be a poor thing, ridden with error, with works fit only to be torn down and put out of the way, still this is my all given to be torn down and put out of the way because my ultimate commitment is devotion to what in truth does bring life to the best, beyond my error and my defeat. This is the only way I can give my life to the power, whatever it be, beyond my understanding, whereby life might be brought to the best attainable. With this confession of faith a final peace is found where no fate can hurt and no disaster destroy.

This basis of faith needs no protection against inquiry, as Barth's does; nor does it depend on the "power of being" inaccessible to intellectual inquiry as Tillich's does. It is exposed to all the assaults of fortune and all the demands of reason. It needs no protection from any of these.

Some seem unable to understand a faith based on *what-*

ever in truth promotes the greater good when this *whatever* is given the name of God. Some seem to think that when you do this you are trying to trick them into a belief in God. This is a total misunderstanding of what is involved. Confessing a religious faith after this manner is not an argument. It is not intended to prove that God must certainly exist because the *whatever* can scarcely be doubted. On the contrary this confession of faith is only a way of uncovering the ultimate foundation of commitment.

Some have said that this *whatever* is a minimum definition of God. This also is a misunderstanding. It is not a definition: it is a way of pointing to the deepest source from which new ventures of faith can forever spring after every error, every defeat and the misadventure of a total life. Some think that when one identifies God with *whatever* he is trying to induce pious people to accept him by using the holy name in this vacuous manner. Still others ask if you are not trying to get everyone to agree with you by affirming a belief in God from which all controversial assertions are removed. All this is misunderstanding. The confession of faith in *whatever* makes for the greater good is not a statement of what one believes God to be. Beliefs about God are reared on this foundation and go far beyond this rudimentary statement.

Many other misunderstandings arise when one makes this confession of faith. Perhaps they come from people who have never found a faith able to endure all doubt, all intellectual inquiry, every challenge of reason and the defeat of a total life's undertaking. There is such a foundation and he who lives the religious life has found it if his faith is truly liberal.

So far we have applied the first of three tests to the Barthian form of faith. This first of the three is the test of reason. The question can always be asked of every affirmation of faith: How is this affirmation related to human reason and all the resources of human inquiry? Must it at some point or other be protected by putting up a barrier against further inquiry? We have found that Barth and Tillich both find it necessary to do this, Barth by wrapping himself in God's grace, Tillich by referring all the last questions to the power of being beyond the reach of all intellectual inquiry.

The second test which every affirmation of faith must meet is the problem of evil. Can it accept the reality of evil in all its depth and magnitude or must it protect itself by denying the reality of evil at some level of being? This test will now be applied to Barth's theology. He writes as follows concerning sin and evil:

. . . this whole realm that we term evil—death, sin, the Devil, and hell—is not God's creation, but rather what was excluded by God's creation, that on which God has said, No. And if there is a reality of evil, it can only be the reality of this excluded and repudiated thing, the thing behind God's back, which He passed over, when He made the world and made it good . . . What is not good God did not make; it has no creaturely existence. But if being is to be ascribed to it at all, and we would rather not say that it is non-existent, then it is only the power of being which arises out of the weight of the divine No. We must not look for darkness in God himself. He is the Father of light. . . . If we begin to speak of *Deus absconditus* we are speaking of an idol. And what is in being, what is in truth real, is by this favour of God. . . . What exists *exists*, because it exists not of itself but by God's Word, for his Word's sake, in the sense and in the purpose of His Word. God upholds all things.

And if we inquire into the *goal* of creation, the object of the whole, the object of heaven and earth and all creation, I can only say that it is to be the theatre of His glory. The meaning is that God is being glorified. . . . We must not desire to know *a priori* what goodness is, or to grumble if the world does not correspond to it. For the purpose for which God made the world it is also good.[7]

These statements about evil are exceedingly evasive. They seem to say one thing and deny it at the same time. It is said that what exists does not exist of itself but only by God's word. Yet sin and evil exist. It is said that they exist behind God's back. What is not good has no creaturely existence. Referring to sin and death he remarks evasively "if being is to be ascribed" he would "rather not say that they are non-existent." One must demand of Barth that he speak forthrightly and say either that sin actually exists or it does not. To say that it exists and yet somehow has a questionable existence, that all things are created and have being only by God's Word and yet to say at the same time that evil has being only by God's No, all these half-assertions indicate refusal to admit the full reality of evil. According to Barth's form of faith, God's goodness and almighty power must be protected by denying full reality to sin and evil.

On page 117 Barth writes that when man sins he "puts himself where God cannot see him." Yet on page 135 we are told that "God knows everything that exists and happens. Then we may well be terrified."

One can justify such affirmations only on the ground that God's grace enables Barth to know that statements contradicting one another are all true. God's grace gives one the freedom to believe what is denied and to deny what is believed. As Barth wrote in a statement previously quoted, one must believe despite contradictions and even identify the contradictions with the devil.

But all this is not fair to Barth. One must see what impels him to view sin and evil in this way. The very foundations of his faith are at stake. His faith is founded on the affirmation that all things have being only by God's Word. If this cannot be held, then all is lost. Therefore Barth is obligated to deal with sin and evil in this gingerly manner, affirming what he denies and denying what he affirms.

Barth is not alone in this predicament. This is the ancient and insoluble problem called the theological problem of evil. It is insoluble because it is a belief affirmed contrary to the evidence. The evidence is the reality of evil in all its depth and magnitude. The belief to be protected is that all things have being only by the power of God who is infinite in love, justice and power. One must stand by the faith to which he has given himself in ultimate commitment. If this requires repudiation of what is known to be true by the rational powers of the mind, then something must be wrong with these rational powers. It may be pride or some other corruption due to sin.

The test here under consideration is one every form of religious faith must meet. It is this: Can faith in God admit the full reality and magnitude of evil and still stand unshaken? It is plain that Barth's form of faith cannot. But there is a faith that can.

The faith fit to meet this test is commitment to whatever the best may be within reach of possible human experience. By no means does this form of faith stop with such an empty affirmation. It goes on to construct beliefs concerning what this best may be, always guided by available evidence. The divine creativity set forth in this writing represents such a belief. But we are now looking at the bottom foundation of faith. The foundation is not this belief because every such belief is liable to error. Nevertheless faith in this creativity does not need to protect itself against the reality of evil, no matter what magnitude evil may have. Commitment to this creativity is unshaken even though evil should overwhelm it. Yet even this kind of commitment is not the last resource.

Belief in this creativity might be mistaken. If that should be so, some other belief will be erected on the foundation of *whatever* makes for the best.

No matter how limited that best may be beyond the reach of our present understanding, supposing that it is other than the divine creativity, still it has all the value which the best can have. Therefore when we commit ourselves to it by way of a belief about it, we have identified ourselves with this greatest good. Suppose it should go down to defeat and cease to be. All this does not diminish in the slightest the value of the good. If the best should have this tragic character, the tragedy of it does not dim the glory of it, whatever that glory may be.

There is no truth whatsoever in the claim that if the good should go down in defeat, man's life committed to it is futile and meaningless. Only worship of the bitch goddess of success can give any semblance of truth to this lie about the meaning and worth of human existence. No matter how brief its time and weak its power before the overwhelming might of evil, to live and die for the greatest good is to have that good in one's own life.

Nothing here stated should be interpreted to mean that the good is weak or will be defeated. Nobody knows enough to make such an assertion. Whether the good will triumph or be defeated, whether it is vastly stronger than evil or the reverse, are beliefs about it; and all these beliefs are liable to error. For example, Bertrand Russell's youthful essay written many years ago when he referred to the slow sure doom of all ideals and human hopes is a prediction about the future. No one knows enough about the future to make any such prediction with certainty.

The foundation of faith here described does not need to be protected by any evasion or fabrication concerning the reality and magnitude of evil. Whatever the evil may be there is a better and a worse. Our responsibility is to seek to know what is better and then commit ourselves to it under the guidance of the most reliable belief we can achieve. Liability to error and uncertainty of the outcome cannot disturb this foundation of faith. Whether the good is mighty or weak over against the evil, it is the best there is and blessedness is found in living for it even in error and defeat. This is the ultimate triumph of faith over evil and over error.

There is still a third test to be met by every form of faith. It has to do with the meaning of history. Of every form of religious faith it can be asked: Does it have the insight and vision to see a great good extending throughout the course of history or must it speculate about what lies beyond history to make the course of events worth while? This test applies to Barth's theology also. Following are some of the statements made by Barth about the meaning of history.

He sitteth on the right hand of God the Father . . . That is . . . the first and last thing that matters for our existence in time. At its base lies this existence of Jesus Christ, His sitting at the right hand of God the Father. Whatever prosperity or defeat may occur in our space, whatever may become and pass away, there is one constant, one thing that remains and continues, this sitting of His at the right hand of God the Father. There is no historical turning-point which approaches this. Here we have the mystery of what we term world history . . . (p. 126)

If the lordship and rule of Jesus Christ at the Father's right hand is the meaning of what we see as the existence of our world-history and our life-history, then this existence of Jesus Christ is not a timeless existence, and eternity is not a timeless eternity. Death is timeless, nothingness is timeless. So we men are timeless when we are without God and without Christ. Then we have no time. But this timelessness He has overcome. Christ has time,

the fullness of time. He sitteth at the right hand of God
as He who has come, who has acted and suffered and tri-
umphed in death. His session at God's right hand is not
just the extract of this history; it is the eternal within this
history. (p. 130)

World history with its industry, with its wars and its
armistices, the history of civilisation with its illusions and
improbabilities—is that a way? We have to smile. But
when He comes, He who is the Actor, then from there all
that is so miserable in our 'Progressiveness' is drawn into
a different light. The frightful folly and weakness of the
Church and of the world are lit up by Him. "Christ is
born." (p. 133)

These quotations when interpreted in the context of
Barth's whole theology make plain that he sees no great good
in any course of events extending throughout human history.
There is nothing intrinsic to these events to make them worth
while. Whatever value they have must be derived from what
is outside of them. They get their value from one event called
the life of Jesus Christ combined with what is not in the
actual events of history at all. This something outside of history is called Jesus Christ sitting at the right hand of God the
Father and coming again at the end of history. Thus according to Barth the actual events throughout the course of history can take on value only by serving what is external to
them. In history taken by itself there is nothing to give it
grandeur, nothing to make it worthy of the devotion and
sacrifice of ultimate commitment. Any claim that history in
itself has such importance causes Barth to say, "We have to
smile."

In contrast to this Barthian view of history is another
view, appearing when ultimate commitment is given to the
divine creativity extending through the events of our temporal existence generation after generation. Constructive criti-

cism of Barth calls for examination of this alternative view.

The word "history" is itself ambiguous and before we can point out the supreme importance of actual events continuing through the sequence of generations we must distinguish three meanings commonly attached to the word "history." According to one meaning the word refers to past events in the life of man. According to another it refers not to the past but to the present, namely to what the historian tells us about the past. History in this sense is always in the present. Even if the book about the past was written many years ago it is history for us only when we read it in the present. History in this sense is the imaginative reproduction of the past by those now living.

History in the third sense is different from both of the two meanings mentioned. It is the consequences of past events in so far as they reach into the present and make us what we are. Books about past events are themselves consequences of past events reaching into the present; but historical writing is only a small part of these consequences. The most important of these is our language. By language is not meant merely verbal sounds and written marks. Rather what is meant is that vast reach of meaning, all that variety of meanings, all that subtle nuance of meaning, carried by linguistic symbols and other symbols also. Under the head of language we wish to include all symbols capable of conveying a meaning from one generation to the next and expanding the range of meaning by receiving additional meaning contributed by each generation.

Language in this sense has been created progressively throughout many thousands of years. It began we know not how with meanings very limited in scope and very few in number. But as generations passed, this scope of meaning, the variety of meanings, the subtlety of meaning, the analytic penetration of meaning, has increased until we have the language used by men today including science and all forms of art.

Most of the events creating this language we now use are unknown. The most originally creative of these events occurred long before any record was made by which we might learn about them. Language began when human life began 200,000 years ago, more or less. The meanings thus created throughout many thousands of years enter into our lives today. Our minds can achieve appreciative understanding of one another in subtlety and depth because we share common symbols with meanings created throughout the course of history. Still more important, the meanings given to us by our language actually create our minds; and it is because our minds have been created in this way that we can understand one another as we do. Love, beauty, power, morals, religion, society, culture, all that is distinctively human in our existence is born anew in each generation by acquisition of these meanings. Our ability to appreciate what is good and distinguish what is evil at the level distinctively human has been in great part created by history.

In addition to language with all its meanings, much else has been produced throughout human history and much of it has destroyed the meanings created by previous generations; much of it has prevented individuals and generations from making the contribution they might. Many historical events have obstructed and beaten down the growth of meaning attached to symbols transmitted through the ages. All this is evil and history is full of it. The consequences of unknown past events would be far more creative of the human mind and personality if these evils had not occurred. But here again it must be repeated: The reality of evil in no wise diminishes the reality of what is good. We are asking: What is the great good to be found in history? We might ask: What is the great evil? It would not be difficult to find horror enough. But we are asking: What is the meaning of history? The word "meaning" here refers to the greatest good produced in history. The word "history" refers to the consequences of past events so far as they reach into the present and make us what we are.

We can now answer the question about the meaning of history. The most valuable product of human history is each individual person so far as he is progressively created from early infancy. The individual is created from infancy by acquiring the meanings of symbols and these meanings are in great part the consequences of past events reaching into the present. When these symbols and their meanings are integrated into the functioning of the biological organism we have the human personality.

The individual is not only progressively created from infancy in this way. He is also stunted, distorted and perverted. The stunting, distorting and perverting should be distinguished from the progressive creation. The stunting and perverting are those consequences of past events which obstruct creative interchange. This is the evil of history.

What is meant by progressive creation of the individual will here again be repeated because our question about the meaning of history will not be clear unless it is again brought to mind. Progressive creation of what is distinctively human in each individual is the increase of five ingredients. These five are not separable parts. They are merged together to form the mind of the individual.

First of these five is expanding the range of what the individual can know, can control, can appreciate as good and distinguish as evil.

The second is increase in appreciative understanding of the unique individuality of oneself and of others. Appreciative understanding includes evaluation of the good and evil in oneself and in others. The standard of evaluation can be stated thus: Goals of endeavor are better or worse according to the measure that they provide conditions favorable for the kind of interchange which creates appreciative understanding of one another.

The third of the ingredients progressively created is progressive integration of personality. The integration must be progressive because new developments are always arising and these will bring on inner conflict if they are not integrated into the unique individuality.

The fourth ingredient in the progressive creation of individuality is ability to encounter creatively defeat, failure, suffering, and prospect of death. To encounter these creatively means to deal with defeat, failure, suffering and prospect of death in such a way that they expand the range of what the individual can know, control, appreciate as good and distinguish as evil. Also, it means to encounter them in such a way that they increase one's appreciative understanding of his own individuality and that of others. Also this encounter is creative when it results in a more powerfully integrated personality. In sum, to meet these dark realities creatively means to deal with them in such a way that they promote, instead of hinder, the progressive creation of all the other ingredients of personality.

The last of the five lines of development included in the progressive creation of human personality is increase of freedom.

The best way to watch history creating its most valuable product is to observe a small child learning to use the language of the prevailing culture when it is tenderly nurtured and other conditions are favorable. The child learning to use the language with all its meanings is history in the making. This is so because history would immediately come to an end if each generation did not acquire the meanings created throughout past generations and transmit them to the future. No event in all the events occurring is so critically important for the continuation of history as the baby learning to talk.

This answer to the question: What is the meaning of history? will be better understood if we compare it with other answers to this question. Some try to answer the question by pointing to an alleged overall pattern into which all the events of history are supposed to fit like pieces of a picture puzzle. Put the pieces together in the right way and you can see throughout the course of history a picture slowly being created which, when completed, will be the Kingdom of God. Others say that a sequence of pictures are created and then destroyed. This is called the rise and decline of civilizations or the cyclical view of history.

Still others try to answer the question by telling of some alleged final outcome to be achieved at the end of history. Marx called this outcome the classless society. Many Christian theologians ridicule Marx but claim to know the outcome of history with even less sustaining evidence than Marx can muster. They call it the second coming of Christ or simply refer to it as "beyond history."

Still others say that no meaning can be found in history until you look at Jesus Christ. But when in faith you accept Christ you can thereafter catch glimpses throughout history of a meaning first discovered in Christ. Paul Tillich and Nicolai Berdyaev answer the question about the meaning of history by saying that historic events symbolize in diverse ways the transcendent fullness of being although this being is not itself historical and is unknowable.

In opposition to all these attempts to find the meaning of history is the meaning found by commitment to the divine creativity. This meaning is revealed in the event of the child acquiring the meanings created by past events. The rearing of empires and nations, laws and constitutions, the development of technologies and economic production, conquests and defeats, migrations and diffusions, great works of art and monuments, none of these reveal the meaning of history. Not until one sees how these bear upon the progressive creation of the individual can he find the meaning of history.

All these constructions contribute to the meaning of history or obstruct it, to the measure that they promote or hinder the progressive creation of each individual.

Alexander the Great at the peak of his power did not do so much for history as did the children in his time who were learning to talk because without the children the achievements of Alexander would not be a part of history today. The children could dispense with Alexander but Alexander could not dispense with the children. The creativity of history would be with us still if Alexander had never lived; but it would not be with us if the progressive creation of human personality beginning with childhood had not occurred.

The kind of interchange creating the mind of the child is identically the same creative interchange which creates history. This is so if we mean by history the consequences of past events reaching into the present to make us what we are. What creates the mind of the individual is what transmits the culture from age to age. This transmission is precisely what is meant when we use the word "history." What creates and sustains history is what creates and sustains the mind of each individual. The creativity operating in the one case is identically the same as the creativity operating in the other case. These are merely different ways of viewing the same creativity.

What obstructs and reduces the volume of history obstructs and reduces the progressive creation of individual personality. The creation of human history in each generation sinks toward extinction just to the measure that the progressive creation of personality sinks toward extinction. Thus human personality and human history are bound together inextricably by the same identical creativity, namely, the kind of interchange between individuals and peoples which does two things: (1) creates appreciative understanding of one another; (2) integrates into each individual and people the knowledge, skill and values thus derived from the other.

Thus do we find God in history when God is the divine creativity. This creativity calls for the ultimate commitment of every person because it creates the individual personality and the whole course of history by the same identical act of creative power. This meaning of history Barth fails to find. He can find nothing in the actual events of history worthy of religious commitment. If you brought a child and set him down in the midst and said, "Behold, the Kingdom of God!", Barth would smile disparagingly, according to his own account of himself, and would point beyond history to Christ sitting at the right hand of the Father. That alone, says Barth, can give any meaning and value to the course of events through history.

So far in this interpretation of history emphasis has been put not on recorded history but on the transmission of the consequences of past events reaching us through the daily interchange between individuals. The work of the historian has been ignored. But the work of the historian has its part to play and this will now be examined.

"The mind must transmute into a present possession the remembrance of its passage through the ages of the world. What was once joy and sorrow must now become knowledge." [8]

The historian gives us knowledge about the past by discovering the meaning conveyed by the symbols used by men in past times. Only as we understand what these symbols meant to the men who conducted their lives by their use can we know life as it was lived in other ages. Every artifact is such a symbol. A tool is a symbol because it represents a course of action and the outcome sought by that course of action. The problem of the historian is to discover what was its meaning for people who used it a thousand or ten thousand years ago. That is the meaning he must recover if he is to know the history of that time. So also buildings, roads, coins, works of art, everything made and shaped by human purpose, is a symbol because it represents ways of acting. It symbolizes hopes and fears, hates and loves and all that total complexity of the mind engaged in making, using, and contemplating. We know the past only to the measure that we can recover that complexity of mind which gave meaning to these objects. This we can never do completely and perfectly any more than we can know the total complexity of the mind of the man with whom we talk day by day. But knowledge of the past and knowledge of the man I meet every day is the same kind of knowledge and must be attained in the same way, namely, by discovering what the symbols mean to the person who uses them. I can know the mind of my friend, my wife, my child, only by learning what his words, his gestures, his tools, his clothes, his house, the road he travels, mean to him. So also can I know the mind of men in ages past in this way. I have historical knowledge only to the measure that I am able thus to give to the artifacts and words they used the same meaning these symbols conveyed to the people who lived then. This recovery of the meaning of symbols, when symbol means everything made, used and contemplated, is never complete and perfect but it can be more or less so. So also knowledge of the mind of my present-day associate is never complete and perfect but it can have degrees of completeness and correctness.

This intuitive leap of imagination by which I discover what symbols mean to the other person living across the street, or having lived in ancient Babylon, is the creativity here identified with the divine presence. We know that we understand one another when the intricate network of conversation and the intricate network of behavior in which we both participate all weave together to form a complicated fabric of meaning and action. This weaving together of words in conversation and this weaving together of actions in behavior is like the weaving together of thousands of threads to make a web. To the measure that the fabric is complete, without holes or raveled ends or lose and dangling threads, we know that we understand in one another not only concepts but also values, feelings, hopes and fears. To the measure that raveled edges and dangling threads do not appear, our appreciative understanding of one another is as complete and perfect as is possible for human beings. Always the web, if carefully examined, will show some raveled edges, some dangling threads, some gaping holes. Since this is the case, everyone carries around in himself a loneliness. But all things good in human life are no less precious because they fall short of absolute completeness and perfection.

The point of all this is to show that knowledge of history and knowledge of contemporaries is the same kind of knowledge. Both are the work of divine creativity combined with human labor and research. In seeking knowledge of men in past times we cannot weave thousands of threads into the fabric of contemporary conversation and behavior in exactly the way we can do it with people living around us today. Yet the gifted historian does gather meanings derived from symbols used in past ages and weave them into the lives we live today so that a seamless web unites the present with the past.

Thus the historian contributes to the creativity of history. By no means does the creativity in history depend entirely on the work of the historian. History would continue even though no records of the past were ever recovered and even though the lives lived long ago were never imaginatively reproduced by historical writing. As said before, history is created in every generation by people acquiring through creative interchange the meanings created by past events even when we have no knowledge of those originating events. But the historian helps the past speak to the present with added clarity and power.

The creativity of God weaves a web of life creating a community reaching back to the beginning of history, gathering all men into a fellowship of communication and extending indefinitely into the future. This divine creativity is forming a community out of all the ages of history. In this community the unknown dead speak to the present and the present speaks to the unknown future. In this community all the generations of men, living and dead, speak to one another. This is the meaning of history revealed to faith when faith is commitment to the divine creativity. This answer to to the question about history stands in contrast to the answer given by Karl Barth.

Three tests have been applied to Barth's form of faith. The first was this: Can his faith meet the demands of reason or must it protect itself from rational inquiry by claiming to have an authority beyond the reach of the natural powers of the human mind?

The second test: Can his faith acknowledge the full reality of evil or must it protect itself by claiming that evil has less reality than the good?

The third test: Can his faith find in the actual events of history a good so great that it calls for ultimate commitment or must he look beyond history to find anything good and great enough to make the devotions and sacrifices of our lives worth while?

Our examination has shown that Barth's form of faith cannot meet these tests. A faith not able to meet the tests of reason, nor admit the full reality of evil, nor find in the actual events of history a good commanding religious devotion, lacks the power to carry men though the storms of existence.

Under very special conditions, Barth's form of faith has the power to triumph over the conditions of life. Barth himself has lived under these special conditions and for him this faith has been sustaining and mighty. These special conditions, taken collectively, are given a name. They are called, by those most favored by these conditions, the grace of God, although this is not what the word "grace" is intended to mean. Specifically these conditions can be described as life lived in a community such as the one in which Barth lived, where a very special religious tradition prevailed. Under these conditions the form of faith declared by Barth may be powerful and sustaining. But it cannot be adequate for people living under different conditions because they cannot have God's grace. They cannot, because God's grace is identical with the conditions mentioned. Barth himself says that this grace comes by way of the church and the church in the form upheld by Barth is identical with the special conditions prevailing round about him. Calling these special conditions the grace of God does not alter the case.

Those of us who do not have this grace of God bestowed upon us must have a faith able to meet the insistent demands of reason, able to admit the full reality of evil and able to find a good continuous throughout human history even though this good is limited to the kind of events called creative interchange. This faith and this creativity must be accessible to all men in order that they may participate constructively in the total enterprise of human life upon this planet. We have reached that stage in human history where a world-wide community of faith has become imperative, not limited to a special set of conditions peculiar to a favored few.

The faith declared by Barth is a local affair. It is not local in the sense of being limited to the locality where Barth lived. The special conditions identified with God's grace can be found in many localities but the faith is a local affair in the sense of being limited to these special conditions. Perhaps Barth himself would admit this since he teaches that his faith is restricted to those elected by God to receive the freedom to believe what other men cannot believe.

CHAPTER SIX

WORLD COMMUNITY ANSWERS

Convulsive changes now occurring in the social order among all the peoples of the earth might lead in any one of three directions. One of these is the road to war. It will not here be considered because no one knows what would result from it. Also it is a direction not likely to be chosen deliberately even though developments beyond control might produce it. That leaves open for consideration the other two alternatives. One of these is world community. The other is a global system operated by bureaucracy, dominated by a ruling group, suppressing individuality and human freedom. This global system will hereafter be called the global mechanism in contrast to world community! World community is defined as the kind of society providing conditions favorable for the creativity which has been the theme of previous chapters.

We shall look at some of the conditions and developments which must be overcome if the global mechanism is to be avoided. Also social processes now developing will be ex-

amined which may lead to world community if rightly followed and directed.

Extensive and profound changes must occur in the American way of life and in our foreign policy if this country is
to be an agent in promoting world community. If these
changes do not occur, American influence will work for the
global mechanism, although this is not the intention nor desire of the American people.[9]

For the first time in the history of the world man is
acquiring that magnitude of power and capacity for change
enabling him to shape the course of life as he decides. But
this he cannot do unless he sees clearly the alternative ways
of life which might be followed. Also he must see those social
processes leading to the one or other alternative, depending
on which are promoted. Futility and failure ensue if he depends solely upon idealism, exhortation, good will and love.
Massive changes in the way of human life will not occur
unless powerful social processes are actually operating in such
a way that idealism can work with them. If idealism does not
work with actually operative social processes, it is not effective.

Passivity on the part of people generally will produce the
global mechanism with a ruling group controlling the use of
wealth and directing the instruments of social control. The
men in power might regulate the growth of population, the
industrial productivity, the propaganda, the unconscious per-
suaders and brain washing techniques so that the vast majority will settle down to a deadening apathy of comfort,
amusement and irresponsible indulgence while the few who
love power more than comfort and amusement operate the
mechanisms of social control. The helpless mass of human
beings will then be controlled like cattle by the system of
global mechanism.

That is the one way in which human history might reach
its culminating point of attainment. The other way is for

mankind to decide definitely with an ultimate commitment never to repudiate the one thing which the human race is good for. That one thing is to be the carriers of creativity to higher levels of existence beyond the reach of our present crude and limited imagination.

The vital question of our time is not American democracy versus Russian communism unless out of this conflict a society can arise in which individuals, more widely and freely than is now the case, can bring the total self into action. The major problem is not full employment and prosperity versus unemployment and recession, *unless* the struggle with this problem can bring forth an organization of industry and commerce in which individuals will exercise responsible power and develop their constructive potentialities. The question which matters most is not wider and freer distribution of power versus concentration of power in the hands of a few, unless some organization of society can open the way for continuous operation of creative interchange.

The greatest danger threatening the world today is an enduring peace with all peoples on the planet living together while a powerful economic machine pours out material goods with increasing abundance by automation, so that everyone has his material wants satisfied to satiation, everyone lives in blooming health with medical care and every pill that the human organism can use, everyone has access to all the pleasures that life can offer, so that the world of men and women can wallow in peace and plenty and contentment, until creativity can do nothing more with this lump of humanity covering the earth.

This is the greatest danger because all history proclaims it. Whenever a people has achieved economic abundance and deliverance from war and the threat of war and has gained access to the biological delights of life with special concentration on the delights of sex, whenever any people has reached this level, the slow sure doom descends. Under such

conditions the creative transformation of the individual bringing his constructive potentialities into action is sacrificed for
comfort and pleasure, for peace and sensuality, and for the
prestige of conspicuous consumption.

Under such conditions there are a few who exploit this
situation so that they can dominate over all the others. The
masses are fed and protected, entertained and flattered, because they serve as material upon which these masters can
exercise their power. But these masters who prefer power to
pleasure and ease do not develop the creative potentialities
of individuality in the people. They even sacrifice creative
development of their own individualities in order to fit into
the mechanism of organization by which power is exercised.

This is the greatest danger because we can see it infect-
ing the American people, now that they have attained more
power and greater economic productivity than any other people. Many have seen this creeping paralysis spreading over
the United States. A few months ago Dorothy Thompson
had a syndicated column speaking of it under the heading,
We are Adrift. THE NATION, a weekly journal in issue
of May 17, 1959, devotes almost the entire issue to statements by students graduating from college and university.
Most of them speak of a deadening apathy due to frustration
of individuality. All of us can mention books and articles and
speeches telling of this danger. The novel, *Catcher in the Rye*
by Salinger, cries and storms about it.

The problem is not so simple as the cliché condemning the
evils of conformity. Conformity with respect to the right
things and for the right purpose is indispensable to any high
attainment. He who does not conform to the rules of syntax
and logic, to the rules of courtesy and the law of the land, to
the appeals for help from those in need, to the methods for
learning to read and write, to spell and to use mathematics,
to reading the best books and consulting reliable authorities
in medicine, law and other specializations where experts alone

can find the way, he who does not conform in these and many other ways, will never develop his potential powers. There is no virtue whatsoever in being odd and non-conformist. There is no possible way for the human being to develop except by learning from other human beings and in this way acquire the resources of the culture in which he lives. Doing this requires a great amount of conformity. The present fad of denouncing conformity has itself become a stultifying conformity. One cannot condemn conformity intelligently and rightly unless he has a fundamental principle with which to distinguish the time and place and kind of conformity necessary for the development of individuality and, in contrast to that, the kind of conformity which prevents its development.

The danger that apathy and irresponsibility will bring on the global mechanism is only one side of the picture. The other side presents a danger equally great. Indeed these two dangers augment one another. The one causes the other and the other causes the one, so that the two together work on one another to build up the global mechanism.

This second danger arises from the vast complexity of advanced social organization controlling the affairs of billions of people all over the earth, when instruments of enormous power must be directed by officials and when these same officials must have the disposition and allocation of wealth greater in quantity than anything ever known in the past. There must be top officials in every organization. When these officials control instruments of gigantic power by way of administrative organization indispensable to the performance of their duties, and when fabulous wealth, not owned by them but produced by society, must be directed by them to meet the needs of the social system, a social mechanism arises unresponsive to the people, unless methods are devised and policies adopted to prevent it. The resulting situation is one in which the top officials become inaccessible to the people who are subject to the system of social control. People at the top deal with one another to dispose of the wealth and exercise power in ways that they see fit. In a society where productive power and wealth will be so great as it will be in the near future, this ruling group will have no need to deny the people comfort and amusement. Indeed it will be to their benefit to do so. They can exercise their power and dispose of wealth in a way to pacify them and thus prevent any challenge to their dominant position. They can feed and care for the people as men feed and care for cattle.

Even when wealth and power and complexity are not nearly so great as they will be in a global system, the kind of social order prevails in New York City where the ruling group deal with one another to dispose of money and power with very little intervention from the populace, except on occasions when the people are aroused. The entire edition of THE NATION, October 31, 1959, is given over to a report by Fred J. Cook and Gene Gleason who have made an extensive and intensive study of the way the affairs of the city are managed. They write:

> The sheer weight of the packed, conglomerate masses, the tremendous size of the bureaucracy that has been created to rule over them, the enormous power wielded by an officialdom feeding on $2 billion annually and controlling many times that many billions in long-term deals and business contracts—all of this operates to dwarf the individual and to divorce him from all control of his fate.
>
> The consequence is inevitable. Today, wherever one goes in New York, wherever one hears protest against injustice, one listens to a baffled public denouncing a great impersonal "they" . . . The use of the omnipresent "they" symbolizes graphically the sharp cleavage between the disparate lives of New York: the lives of the congested and struggling and essentially helpless millions, and the

lives of an official and business aristocracy which has lost virtually all of its old connections with the grass roots.

These generalizations are documented in the report by detailed accounts of actual happenings, naming the individuals, localities and organizations involved. This condition is not inevitable, although it does automatically develop unless social organization, methods and policies are adopted to prevent it. Above all, a positive, constructive goal of human attainment must be set forth, widely recognized and accepted, and made a matter of religious commitment. So long as corrective social action has only the negative goal of removing the evil and is not motivated by a positive aim of human attainment, the improvement will be temporary. The direction of human development must be clearly envisaged and persistently sought by institutions and organizations permanently operative and driven by rituals of religious commitment. If this does not prevail, the oppressive mechanism will revert again to its old ways after each popular outburst. After yielding to transitory and superficial reform, the old system will settle back again with more power than ever to resist the popular outcry because the men in power will have learned how to forestall these revolts. Furthermore, a well established global mechanism will be far more inaccessible to the people than is the system in New York. Also it will have wealth and power to keep the people comfortable, entertained and diverted. Intractable individuals who have the drive for power and the competence can be admitted into the ranks of the ruling group, or they can be liquidated.

The United States might become a powerful agent in promoting world community *if the required changes are made*. But the changes must occur if our weight is to be thrown on the side of world community and against global mechanism. Exposing the danger which lies in our present way of life is not defeatism. It is a call for the needed change.

It is with this purpose that the following statement is quoted from the St. Louis Post Dispatch for November 3, 1959. It is quoted not because the speaker is a final authority. Many others have expressed the same conviction in various ways when they have been placed where they can view objectively the conduct of American life and see it in relation to the social developments now occurring over the planet. Walter Lippmann for example has voiced the same view as the one here.

> Professor George Kennan summed up the American dilemma in words which encompass many phenomena: "If you ask me—as a historian let us say—whether a country in the state this country is in today: with no highly developed sense of national purpose, with the overwhelming accent of life in personal comfort and amusement, with dearth of public services and a surfeit of privately sold gadgetry, with a chaotic transportation system, with its great urban areas being gradually disintegrated by the headlong switch to motor transportation, with educational system where quality has been extensively sacrificed to quantity, and with insufficient social discipline even to keep its major industries functioning without grievous interruptions—if you ask me whether such a country has, over the long run, good chances of competing with a purposeful, serious and disciplined society such as the Soviet Union, I must say that the answer is "no."

Great changes will occur in the American way of life in the near future, whether we like it or not. These changes will be driven first of all by the competition becoming ever more intense for world supremacy with the communist countries. The change will also be caused by the need to change our ways in order to exercise control over the gigantic instruments of power which we are developing along with the rest of the world. These instruments of power, becoming ever more powerful, are (1) scientific research, (2) application of this research to technology, (3) education, (4) industrial production, (5) the political mechanism required to control and develop these instruments of power.

There is no question about the changes occurring and the causes producing them. But when this is admitted the question of crucial importance arises. It is this: Will the changes be controlled and directed by a constructive aim concerning what should be the way of life for man? If there should be no such aim, if the changes should occur merely because forced by the developments mentioned, without religious commitment to the creativity for which man is made, the outcome will be the global mechanism, at least so far as the influence of America may reach. Some other peoples might work to save us from that fate, but the influence of the United States would be in the direction of the global mechanism even when our aspirations would be opposed to it.

So long as we use our wealth and power to help the underdeveloped countries and other peoples with the dominant aim to stop communism but without constructive purpose beyond this, or if our purpose be merely to raise their standard of living, or merely to win their friendship and good will, or merely to induce them to approximate the American way of life, or if our purpose be any combination of these, we are headed for defeat both in the competition with communism and in the endeavor to save the world from the global mechanism. This is so because none of these aims includes what is necessary to develop the constructive potentialities of human life by providing conditions favorable for the creativity operating in creative interchange between persons and peoples.

No nation in the future can exist independently of the rest of the world. Every people will be compelled to fit into a world system, compelled not by military conquest but by the spread of economic, political, scientific, technological and educational connections and the way of life resulting from all this. What is meant by the "way of life resulting" can be suggested by saying that the time will shortly come when many a man will start from home in the morning, fly to any remote part of the earth and return by night or next day to his home again.

Just now nationalistic aspirations are more intense than ever before. There are good reasons why this should be, but it cannot long continue without forming international unions. These nationalistic aspirations drive to competition, and international competition, like competition between industrial organizations, compels the formation of unions for strength in the competition. So we see rising far and near the Council of Europe, the Coal and Steel Community, the Federation of West Indies, the United Arab Republic, the Federal Union of Malaya. Even NATO and SEATO might develop international strength. Even the beginning of bonds of union are forming between United States and Russia and United States and China, forced by the necessity for international teams of inspection to guard against nuclear tests and need for other international regulations to control the ever increasing might of instruments of power. These instruments of power can be controlled by nothing less than an earth-encircling system.

This brings us to the question: What must be done to prevent this world system from becoming a global mechanism? What must be done to direct the changes now occurring toward the formation of a world community.

First of all, two fatal illusions must be corrected which seem to be almost universal. One is the illusion that the proper use of leisure will be our problem when the work of economic production and distribution no longer require many man hours. This illusion arises from the notion that when economic work is no longer required beyond a minimum there will be no other work to take its place. This error must be corrected. There will be other work to do, just as insistent as economic work has been throughout human history up to this time. This other kind of work will be the solving of social and interpersonal problems in a way to develop and sustain world community and prevent development of a global mechanism. This work will demand the services of every one at his level of competence, to the same measure that economic work in the past has involved all the people. A few items entering into this social work will be mentioned to indicate something of its character. The six following suggestions make no pretense to being comprehensive.

(1) Billions of money and tens of thousands of men must be devoted to research to learn how to rear a child from infancy so that he will not acquire the suppressions and inner conflicts at that level of the unconscious which obstructs the development and exercise of his creative powers. It has been the fate of all the children, some more and some less, to be blocked in their development by the way they are treated by adults responsible for their care.[10] The consequence of this mistaken care of infants and children is appalling. Human beings have only a fraction of the creativity they would have if they had been reared in a way to develop and exercise their constructive capacity. This wrong treatment produces destructive behavior. Sometimes it is psychologically self destructive or inhibiting; sometimes it is socially destructive; sometimes it results in apathy; sometimes all these in various combinations.

(2) To the measure that research finds out how to rear infants and small children in a way to preserve and develop their capacity for creative interchange, all parents should be required to study continuously under instruction to learn what this research has discovered. Parents should be required to do this by being paid for it just as though they were working for General Motors or the Steel Industry or doing any

work which in the past has received pay. It should be understood that the parents are earning part of their living by this kind of study so that, if they do not make the grade in this work, they will be unemployed in this area of employment with consequent diminution of their income. In other words, rearing children should be understood to be work as important as producing economic goods. It might be necessary to limit the number of children parents can have, ranging from none to a few or more, depending on whether they can show that they have learned how to care for children. "Care for children" here refers not merely to bodily care but primarily to psychological care. It will be necessary to limit population in some way and this might be one procedure.

This kind of study and education should be established as the work by which human life is sustained at the level of creativity demanded by existence distinctively human. This kind of work, even though it might be highly enjoyable, is no more a form of leisure than raising wheat or running a service station to keep the automobiles going. To keep human life going at a high level of creative interchange is no less important than keeping the automobile going.

The illusion here to be corrected is the notion that work is limited to production and distribution of economic goods and that education and rearing children is not work. We are moving into a time when the most important work for all humanity will be its education, continuing throughout the entire life of the individual. We are coming to the time when food and shelter will no longer be the problem. The problem will be to educate people with that extensive and intensive thoroughness required to sustain a World Community and save humanity from the degradation of a global mechanism.

(3) Billions of money and thousands of men are now being used for research in the natural sciences and in the work of applying the findings of the natural sciences to the tech-

nologies of industry and war. If we are to have a world community, even more billions of money and thousands of men must be applied to research in the social sciences to help solve the problems of life at the levels of psychological organization, social organization and historic continuity. This will require not only trained scientists but also millions of helpers at all levels of competence. This use and development of research in the social sciences has been held back partly by the immaturity of these fields of inquiry. Even more it has been held back by lack of clarity on what we want to achieve by way of developing personality, social interchange and historical continuity. Once it is understood what to seek by this inquiry, the social sciences can make invaluable contribution to the conduct of human life. Once there is clarity and agreement on the purpose to be attained, the powers of research can show the way to its attainment. The present writing is an attempt to state what this purpose should be.

So far research in the social sciences has been used to serve special interests by way of propaganda, advertising, and the like. The comprehensive goals of human existence have been excluded from consideration by this research because the goals of special interests in industry, politics and war have been the only ones sufficiently defined to be served. This perversion of research can be corrected only when the comprehensive goal of human existence is sufficiently well defined to show the problems to be solved by research. When this is done, great advances might be made and innumerable people might be employed in this service, leaving the production and distribution of economic goods largely to automation and the limited number of man-hours required.

(4) To the measure that research finds how the many complex social problems should be treated to sustain a world community, all adults should study these problems under competent instructors; and this study should not end until the individual has reached the age of retirement. Here again

the individual should be paid and should pursue this study as the work by which he earns his living. If he stops or fails to learn what is required, he will be unemployed in this area of occupation and his income will be restricted by that much.

Work is doing what is necessary to sustain civilization. The only reason we call economic production "work" is because it is necessary to sustain society at a level and in a form acceptable to human beings. For precisely the same reason and with exactly the same definition of work, the kind of education here suggested is work. It is indispensable work when indispensable means what must be done if a civilization of free men is to survive. Since it is necessary work it should receive remuneration like any other kind of work.

Some will ask: Where can we get the money to pay for work which is not economic production? In reply I again refer to the examination of this very problem by a competent economist. John K. Galbraith in *The Affluent Society* devotes the entire volume to showing the dangerous "social unbalance" in our society from failure to devote a far greater part of our wealth to public services such as education. He also demonstrates that this social unbalance can be corrected by providing education and other public service in such a way as not to reduce economic production but to stabilize and increase it. I shall not here attempt to report the facts and arguments of this book. I must leave the problem in the hands of expert economists such as the author of the volume mentioned. I only report from this economist and others that three dangers threaten our economy. They are inflation, the creation of demand for goods by frantic advertising and installment buying, and the social unbalance resulting in lack of social services of which education is chief. Providing these services in the right way will not reduce but will aid the production of economic goods by guarding against these dangers.

(5) A further kind of work should not be confused with

leisure and should be paid when economic work is no longer demanded of the persons concerned. It is research to find how to diversify education in a way to fit the needs of individuals so that their capacities can be developed. At present we set up an educational system for everyone, demanding that each individual be run through the same mill. But the same teacher who is best fitted to educate one individual is not fitted to meet the needs of another. The methods and subject matter which can bring one individual to the peak of achievement will leave another scarcely awakened from the torpor resulting when he is not interested or incapable of understanding. This is not merely a difference in ability. It is difference in what is required to educate effectively different individuals. Winston Churchill was a very poor student in school, not because he was unfit for education but because the educational system then and there in operation was unfit for him. The same was true for Charles Darwin. These two individuals were fortunate to find ways to educate themselves when the schools failed to provide what their individualities needed. But there is every reason to believe that millions are never developed to a high level because the teachers, methods and materials in the established system of education have been unfit to awaken their powers.

(6) To the measure that research of this kind discovers how to diversify teachers, methods and materials to meet the needs of diverse individuals, millions of teachers, administrators, librarians, organizers, inventors and constructors of equipment will be needed to provide this diversified kind of education. This again is not a form of leisure. It is one kind of work which will absorb the man-hours released from business, industry and agriculture. Heretofore we have proceeded on the notion that when the bed provided by the educational system did not fit the individual, we should chop off his legs or pull them out to the length of the bed. We may in time wake up to the realization that it is much more

intelligent to fit the bed to the individual, rather than chop him down or pull him out to fit the bed. But diversified education of this sort will require far more man-hours of teaching, administration and other services than a standardized system requires.

What we have been trying to demonstrate under points (1), (2), (3), (4), (5), (6) is that work hereafter must be identified with education and the application of this education to the problems of social existence, whether it be the social existence of the infant and small child, or the interpersonal relations of husband and wife and children, or the social existence of diverse groups and cultures sustaining relations in which each can gain appreciative understanding of the needs and interests of the other and learn from the other without imposing uniformity upon all. All this education will make possible the further work of developing and continuously modifying the basic institutions of society so that they will provide social conditions under which the individual can engage in creative interchange with associates; and peoples can do the same with one another.

The fatal fallacy to overcome if anything like this is to happen is the fallacy about leisure. If the fallacy persists that release from economic work means leisure and not a different kind of work, as imperative as economic production ever was, there will be no escape from the fate threatening to suppress the individual and degrade humanity to the point where not enough initiative, imagination and trained intelligence will be left to preserve order and provide comfort for the billions swarming over the planet. When that time comes and the whole system collapses either by gradual stagnation or mob violence, the human story will come to an end. It will come to an end because in that time the instruments of destruction will be universally annihilating. But it need not turn out that way. It will not turn out that way if people learn to recognize work when they see it and establish the institutions to provide it. The kind of work must be the work of continuous education from infancy to old age, with the continuous application of that education to the problems of social existence.

There will always be some leisure, just as there has been in the past. That point is not disputed. What is disputed is the claim that there will be more leisure in the future than there is today. There will be more leisure in the future only if men refuse to undertake the kind of work which must be done if humanity is to be saved from degradation by a global mechanism. Also it is not here disputed that economic work in production and distribution of goods and services must always be done so long as human life continues. It is only claimed that this kind of work will be a diminishing part of the total work which men must do to sustain human life.

Besides the illusion about leisure there is another illusion calling for correction. It may not be as dangerous as the fatal fallacy about leisure but it can be very serious. It is the notion that what is now called communism will continue to be ruled by a dictatorship so harsh and unjust that no world community can be formed bringing the communist countries and the Western world together in brotherhood. This obstruction to any world community calls for examination.

The first thing to understand about tyranny whether in Russia or anywhere else is to see that it is never the work merely of a group of conspirators who want supreme power. Neither is the continuance of a dictatorship determined by the will of those in power to retain arbitrary might. Tyranny in all cases can arise only when social conditions permit. So also democracy can arise and prevail only when social conditions permit it. When social conditions do not permit democracy, some other kind of government will exercise control, if any government at all can operate.

Let us look at the social conditions which brought forth

dictatorship in Russia. We shall see that these conditions are rapidly changing so that conditions coming to prevail in Russia no longer support the kind of arbitrary power exercised by the Russian government in the past. This means that the dictatorship of the past cannot continue, not because the men in power want to relinquish their power, but because social conditions do not permit them to exercise power in the way it was done under Stalin.

Five conditions prevailed in Russia giving rise to tyranny and all of them are disappearing. The first was the heritage from the Czars and the Tatars. Russia for centuries had been ruled by tyranny. Consequently the habits and expectations of the people, the training and competence of administrators, the entire structure of society reaching down into the unconscious attitudes of all the people, were adapted to tyranny. It is impossible to change all that in any society within less than a generation. Consequently when the communists came into power the entire society was set and ready for tyranny and could not have operated under any other kind of government. Lenin tried to introduce some measures of democracy but found that he could not make them effective.

A second condition which brings on tyranny is swift and revolutionary change in ownership of property and industrialization of society. We speak of the American revolution but it was not this kind of revolution. It is impossible to take property away from the people who own it and industrialize the economy at furious speed except by ruthless methods of coercion. This is no justification for ruthless method. It is simply a report of the actual conditions and what actually happened. The report is here made in order to show that these conditions are rapidly disappearing in Russia. The property has already been taken from private ownership and a generation has arisen that never owned productive property. Rapid industrialization in Russia has reached the point where it can go on without basic change in the economic structure of society because the society now has institutions established and habits formed which are adapted to rapid industrialization. For a generation after 1917 this adaption had to be more or less coerced. It has now become more or less the established and accepted system.

A third condition prevailing in Russia which forced the concentration of supreme power in a central agency was the threat of attack from powerful enemies. Russia since the revolution has lived in this fear and has been attacked and invaded. Invasion occurred during the first years after 1917 and also when Germany attacked under Hitler. The people and the rulers have always been under fear of attack and such fear always leads to highly centralized control. It does it in the United States. We have a built-in system by which supreme power is given to the president in time of war, making him commander in chief of a military organization.

This fear of attack no longer operates to uphold tyranny in Russia as once it did because the rulers and the people feel, as the United States feels also on its side, that it has the power to counter attack with such devastation that no enemy will dare turn loose the dogs of war. Furthermore, readiness for war no longer requires control of a massive army and hence military organization of all the people. Rather it requires control over atomic missiles and the experts who operate them.

A further condition prevailing in Russia up until the recent past which invited tyranny was the danger of counter revolution. This is always present after the kind of revolution which occurred in Russia in 1917. The people of wealth and power who are dispossessed, and many others who resist swift and violent change in their ways of life, plot and scheme and organize to overthrow the revolutionary regime. Most revolutions have been overthrown because of this. The only way to resist this counter revolution is to exercise dictatorial power with an elaborate system of spies or secret police. We have developed such a system ourselves, called the Central Intelligence Agency and the F.B.I. But the danger of subversion has been much greater in Russia than it ever was in the United States.

This danger of subversion which was one of the causes for dictatorship, has greatly diminished in Russia. So this is another cause of tyranny no longer operative as once it was.

Finally the condition prevailing in Russia which supported tyranny was the lack of education on the part of the masses of people. Excepting a very small minority, the Russians were not educated in a way to understand the problems of their society and could not exercise initiative, control and responsibility in the conduct of affairs. Today everyone in Russia who is old enough to go to school has done so; and great numbers are highly trained and quite competent to exercise management in many different areas of society. Indeed a complex and highly industrialized society such as Russia has now become would break down if there was not wide distribution of power and responsibility. This does not mean that Russia is acquiring or ever will acquire our kind of democracy. But tyranny in the sense of concentrated power in the hands of a few is no longer possible. The supreme ruler in Russia can dominate as he cannot do in the United States, but he cannot exercise power arbitrarily when so many highly competent men exercise great power and responsibility under him throughout wide regions of the complex society.

This survey of the causes making possible the dictatorship in Russia, and the decline of these conditions, so that the dictatorship of the extreme type is no longer possible, shows that the tyranny of Russia is not an unchanging obstacle in the way of developing a world community.

The notion that communism will always be an insuperable barrier to world community is derived in part from the famous statement made by Khrushchev referring to the world supremacy to be gained by communism over against the Western democracies. His statement was: We will bury you.

This statement points to the competition between communism and the Western world. This competition will continue and perhaps become increasingly intense. Furthermore it will result in producing a world system and this system will bury the social system now prevailing in Russia. It will also bury the social system now prevailing in the Western world. It will be a social system very different from anything now called communism and very different from anything now called Western democracy.

I do not know if Khrushchev understood the true significance of his own assertion. This true significance, which in all probability Khrushchev did not intend, is completely misunderstood if one thinks it means that the communist system as it now exists will prevail over the American system as it now exists. All such notions are based upon the false idea that the communist system will continue unchanged or will follow the course of change predicted by Marxism until it either wins or loses in the competition for world supremacy. The idea is equally false that the American system will remain unchanged or follow the course of predicted change until it either wins or loses in the competitive struggle. These are both illusions. Both are contrary to all the evidence we have concerning the development of social systems.

The so-called communist system of Russia has been undergoing radical and unpredicted changes since it was initiated by Lenin. Never has it been changing more rapidly, radically and unpredictably as now. These changes are forced by competition with the Western world in the effort to produce more goods; to exercise more political power throughout the world; to influence and persuade more people in Asia and Africa and South America; to educate everybody more intensively so that all the people can cooperate effectively in the rapid industrialization of the country; to extend and intensify scientific research and apply it most quickly to the technology of the country; to develop all the instruments of power provided by modern civilization and apply them to ends sought. These are the forces compelling and directing the course of change in Russia. These changes do not follow the line prescribed by Marxist theory. Also change is forced by the necessity to cooperate with the Western world to avoid atomic war, to stop nuclear tests, to bring about disarmament so far as possible, to resolve points of dangerous conflict in many parts of the world, to maintain that kind of interchange of scientists and scientific knowledge without which science cannot continue in the way it must continue if Russia is to hold her own in the competition.

What has just been said about the world of communism applies in like manner to the United States and the Western world. American democracy has undergone radical changes since it was initiated by George Washington, Alexander Hamilton and Thomas Jefferson; and never has it changed more rapidly, radically and unpredictably than it is now changing under the stimulus of competition with communism. We undergo change in order to exercise more political power, to influence and persuade more people, to educate everybody more intensively so that all the people can cooperate in devising, constructing and operating the instruments of power put into the hands of man by modern civilization.

Since this competition together with other conditions is causing the communist system to change continuously, radically and unpredictably, and also causing the American system to do likewise, what will come out of it will not be the dominance of the American system in the form in which it now exists. Neither will it be the communist system in the form it now exists nor in the form predicted by Marxian theory. What kind of social order will finally emerge out of this competition no one knows. But two things we can know. We can know that the competition between the two systems may cause both to seek a social order which will develop the creative potentialities of men by way of creative interchange because such a system will win over any other if it is developed. Secondly, we can know that the struggle to develop and control such instruments of power as science, technology, education and industrial production will lead to world community rather than a global mechanism if the participants are intelligent enough to develop the kind of society which can magnify and control these instruments most effectively.

On the other hand it is quite possible that a global mechanism will bury all of us. If the mistaken notion persists that the alternative to economic work is leisure and if the equally mistaken notion continues that communism as it now exists is an insuperable obstacle to community with the Western democracies, we are headed for a fate which may grind out of us the high gift distinguishing man from every other animal. That gift is the divine creativity. Whether the social processes now developing move in the direction of a global mechanism or a world community depends in no small part on decisions made by the people of the world. Not least among the peoples required to make this decision are the American people. No decision is more fateful than what we decide to do in dealing with people of the communist world. Shall we oppose and try to dominate or shall we seek creative interchange with them?

The struggle to develop and control the instruments of power above mentioned will lead to a world community if we are successful in our endeavor to control them. Science, for example, is one of these instruments of power. Science demands world-wide interchange among scientists and cannot develop satisfactorily if obstacles are put in the way of this kind of scientific world community. The various branches of research are becoming so highly specialized that individual scientists and specialized groups of scientists are frustrated if they cannot get the knowledge and suggestions from other scientists over the world when these are relevant to the problems on which any one scientist or group of scientists is working. Science has become a vast cooperative system made up of innumerable specialized studies demanding world-wide interchange between individuals and groups. Science is an instrument of power upon which all other instruments of power depend. No people can keep up with the rest of the world if it does not develop science. Hence all the peoples seek it and will have it. But it cannot be developed and operated effectively by any people if that region obstructs world-wide interchange between its scientists and all others. So imperative is this demand of science that it breaks through the barriers set up by governments and by popular prejudice.

Another instrument of power is industrial production and distribution of goods and services. These powers have now become so great, and the demand of impoverished people for the wealth produced has become so insistent, that the economic system cannot operate effectively without world-wide interchange of goods and services together with the world-wide spread of industrial technology. This means interchange informing all people of each new method or other invention to increase productive power and to render distribution more effective in feeding back into the productive process the wealth needed to increase its power. The economic demands of this productive system, by developing all over the world, is breaking down the barriers of prejudice and other obstructions to interchange. For example, powerful forces are gathering strength with the demand that barriers be removed from economic exchange with China although popular sentiment and government in the United States are against it. West Germany cannot be restrained from economic dealing with the communist world and this volume of trade is bound to grow because it brings wealth and power and builds up a nation's influence throughout the world.

Still another instrument of power in the world today

cannot be developed effectively without world-wide interchange. Perhaps this instrument of power is the source of all
other power, even that of science. It is education. Education
has become one of the indispensable means to power in the
world today and all the nations of the world are seeking
power avidly. No man today can be educated in a way to
serve his own society if he does not know about the rest of
the world. He must know other cultures besides his own. He
must know how people feel and think and act in these other
cultures, else he cannot serve his own society. Since education is always designed to serve the society which provides
the education, it is plain that education today requires a
community of interchange between the peoples of the world.
Consequently students are exchanged, teachers are exchanged,
works of art are exchanged, cultural resources in all their
diverse forms are exchanged. All people are eager to learn
about other cultures, because the aim of education cannot
be reached in any other way.

Thus we see that the social process creating world community is being forced upon every people and nation by
the struggle to build up in each nation its own power in
competition with other nations and peoples. I repeat, this
does not mean the inevitable creation of a world community. Other developments are at work which move in the
other direction. The point of this analysis is to show that
social processes are developing with which we can work in
striving to attain a world community. But passivity will not
bring it about. Passivity will result in the opposite. There
must be definite decision, definite commitment and clear
vision of what we seek to achieve.

Society as it moves through history can be compared to
a caravan coming occasionally to a high mountain range over
which it cannot go except by way of a steep and narrow and
stony mountain pass. If it gets over that pass it may enter a
land more opulent than the land through which it has been

traveling. If it does not get over the pass, it will either die at the foot of the mountain range or retrace its steps, returning to the more primitive conditions from which it has come. This situation is what Arnold Toynbee calls challenge and response. It is the way in which every civilization has advanced. Furthermore every civilization has broken down and declined whenever it has come to such a problem requiring a reorganization of society beyond its capacity to change. When a society is able to solve such a problem it generally develops more power to persuade, to create a culture, to produce and to rule. All history, according to Toynbee, is the story of societies coming to a high mountain range over which they could not go without reorganization and developing a higher order. When and if they fail to do this, either they perish or go back to more primitive ways of life.

Today all the societies of the earth are coming to the foothills of a high mountain range. The only way to go over this range is to develop a world community. If we fail, we shall lapse into a global mechanism gradually forcing humanity to levels of degradation from which it may never recover. Yet there is a way of salvation marked out for us by the divine creativity at work in human life. Religious commitment to this creativity opens the way of salvation from the spiritual death of global mechanism; and it opens the way to the spiritual life of a world community.

CHAPTER SEVEN

EDUCATION ANSWERS

The primary responsibilities of education point to what ought to be its aims. So we begin by asking, What are the primary responsibilities of public, institutional education?

The first responsibility is to enable the student to understand the basic problems which must be continuously solved to some degree and in some way in order to sustain civilization. To the measure that these problems are not solved civilization declines. If they were not solved at all to any degree, human life itself would disappear.

For example, the economic problem is one which must be continuously solved to sustain society. It might be worded thus: How produce and distribute goods and services in such a way that the economic system will feed back into the productive process to sustain and preferably increase productive power.

To see the responsibility of education for this problem a sharp distinction must be made between two things. If this distinction is not made with clarity and emphasis, the work of education will be misdirected, as indeed it often is. The distinction is between (1) teaching the student to adopt the beliefs, practices and purposes of the dominant economic institutions of his society and (2) helping the student to understand the basic economic problem which these beliefs and practices are intended to solve.

The student will ordinarily adopt the beliefs, practices and purposes of the dominant economic institutions. There is nothing wrong in this and he should be informed concerning these practices. But there is an enormous difference between adopting a total system of belief and practice without understanding the basic problem which it is intended to solve and adopting it with this understanding. The responsibility of education is to see to it that when the student enters the business world he will understand the problem which must be solved by business practice if the society is to endure and prosper.

If the student adopts the economic way of life in his society without understanding the social problem involved, he cannot act intelligently in playing his part in the economic system. If he does not understand the problem he may become a blind partisan of the established order in disregard of its defects. He may even promote its self destructive propensities without knowing what he is doing. In other cases he may become a rebel against the prevailing system but blind in the sense of not understanding the problem which any economic system must solve if it is to uphold any society. In such case his rebellion, no matter how good his intentions, will be entirely destructive. Or again, if the student does not understand the problem which the system must solve in some way or other, he will engage in business for what he thinks is personal gain, but in such a way as to undermine the economic foundations of the society. This society gives to his wealth all the value it can ever have for him.

Powerful economic institutions might provide money and

have teachers selected on condition that the students be taught first of all to adopt the economic practices of these dominant corporations. This might be done very sincerely and with high moral purpose because the individuals operating these established institutions were never taught to understand the economic problem apart from the practice of the corporations. They may be highly competent and may thoroughly understand the problems involved in operating the established system. But this is not at all the same as understanding the economic problem in the interests of the whole society.

The economic problem of society can be solved in many different ways. Some of these ways are better than others, depending upon the conditions prevailing in that society and in the world generally. The dominant economic institutions do not necessarily provide the best solution of the problem. They might, but the mere fact that they happen at the time to be dominant is not evidence that they do. Furthermore, even if the big corporations do provide the best economic structure for that society, the established system will not be operated in the way best fitted to solve the economic problem for society if the individuals operating the system do not understand the problem from the standpoint of social existence. They are likely to see the problem only from the standpoint of what best serves the interests of the corporation. It is the responsibility of education to enable them to see it more comprehensively and in wider context. Trained blindness can result from high competence in operating an economic institution when there is little understanding of the social function of that institution. Economic theory, when properly taught in college and university, can correct this blindness.

When education does not intervene, the basic problems which must be solved to uphold civilization are viewed as problems solved. Indeed they *are* solved by the beliefs, practices and institutions of the society, for otherwise the society could not continue in existence. But they are never completely and perfectly solved. Human life is always far below what it might be if they were more adequately treated. Not infrequently a society is in process of disintegration without anybody knowing it because no one discerns the problems. This blindness is due to established beliefs and practices and working institutions creating the illusion of problems solved, thereby concealing the problem to be solved. For this reason theory must break through the crust of habit and expose the problem. This is what education should do whether it be the problem of economics or politics or literature or religion. The student must become acquainted with theories concerning how to solve the problem apart from established practice. Otherwise blindness will possess the minds of those who should correct the evil.

The responsibility of education for the economic problem upon which civilization depends is here discussed not because this problem is any more important than a number of others upon which the existence of human society depends. We have discussed it only to explain and illustrate what is meant by the primary responsibility of education relative to the foundations of civilization.

The problem of government is another problem which must be solved in some way and to some degree if civilization is to endure. It might be stated thus: How concentrate supreme power in a central agency in such a way that it will protect the society from external enemies, will maintain order within the society and will have power to do what no other agency is powerful enough to do when the needs of society so require, and do all this in a way to provide freedom for the individual.

Here again the same danger threatens which we have seen in the case of economics and it is the responsibility of education to avert it. The danger is that vision and talent will be directed so exclusively on operating the established system of government that theory concerning how government should serve society will be inaccessible to the minds of men. Yet the principle still stands: Practice without theory is blind.

The teacher is always tempted to laud the government and all its ways to inspire loyalty and devotion in the student. He is also tempted to be "practical" by limiting his efforts to informing the student concerning the actual operative system of government instead of teaching the theory of government. Yet loyalty to the government in disregard of what the government might do but does not do to serve society, is disloyalty to the homeland, not to speak of humanity generally. Also efficiency in operating the established system without regard to the function and the theory of government, is inefficiency in serving society. Thus if the teacher yields to the temptation mentioned, he will be teaching disloyalty and inefficiency while intending to do the opposite.

Literature is another basic problem for which education should assume responsibility. The problem which literature must solve if civilization is to endure might be stated thus: How expose the passions and powerful drives in human life which are concealed by social conventions and the decorum of polite society. These are concealed from consciousness because they are unacceptable to the established order. These passions are concealed even from the consciousness of the individual who has them. On the other hand these passions are presented in false and distorted form by stories and plays and other forms of art which fall short of doing what art in all its forms ought to do. These drives suppressed and concealed because the social order has no place for them must be revealed in some way in order that we may understand ourselves and human beings generally. This is the social function of art and especially of great literature.

Here again we find the blindness which should be corrected by education. The blindness is created by the prevailing and approved forms of art, especially the most popular forms of it. Another name for this blindness is uncultivated and degraded taste. A great part of the entertainment given on radio and television in United States today, offered in order to reach the greatest number of people for the advertisers, is an example of this blindness to the true function of art. It is another example showing how the established and approved way of solving the problem conceals the problem to be solved. Not only in economics and politics and government, literature and art but also in religion, the established system of belief and practice conceals what should be done to save society and the individual from degradation.

This concealing of the problem by the established ways can be compared to a bridge over which people pass continuously. People go back and forth without awareness of the problem involved in constructing a bridge over the torrent. This might continue until change in stream and contour of the land made it impossible to pass over on the bridge as presently constructed. If protection and livelihood depended on getting to the other side of the torrent, the people and their culture might not survive.

This is a parable designed to set forth the primary responsibility of education for the basic problems of society. The primary responsibility is not to teach the students how to operate the established system whether in economics or politics. Neither is it to teach them to create great literature or other art. These accomplishments might very well result from education. But to produce them is not the primary responsibility of education. Education is not called upon to construct a better way of solving these basic problems nor even to urge that a better way be found. Any or all of these might occur as a consequence of the education received; but none of these desirable consequences should obscure the important thing which education must do and which no other agency can do so well.

The important thing is to overcome the great blindness. When the established system conceals the problem to be solved, the civilization where that occurs will disappear if the blindness is not corrected. The established ways are partial, imperfect and temporary solutions of the problems on which society depends. When conditions change, as they always do in time, these established ways will no longer be able to solve the problem sufficiently to sustain the society. In such a time the people should understand the problem so that they can undertake a new solution fitted to their situation. It is the responsibility of education to provide this understanding.

We are living in a time when social institutions are being reconstructed. We should understand the problem which these institutions must solve if civilization is to endure and if man is to be saved from degradation and destruction. The more complex the society, the more rapid the social change and the more power for good and evil exercised by men, the more imperative it becomes that participants in the economic system, in the political order, in the arts and in religion, understand what these practices should do to sustain civilization and the good of human existence.

Perhaps nowhere is the blindness here under consideration so complete as in the conduct of religious living. Even sophisticated philosophers look upon religion as nothing more than a system of belief, feeling and practice, important to the individual and his religious fellowship. No problem is recognized which religious practice must solve in some way or other if human life is to be sustained and the greater good attained. This problem is incompletely, imperfectly and temporarily solved by the great religions. Each of these religions in its own culture provides a very inadequate and unsatisfactory solution. Furthermore with advancing civilization the ancient religion becomes increasingly inadequate to its basic function. The convulsions and disruptions of our time show that the established forms of religion do not solve the problem as it must be solved if these difficulties are to be surmounted.

Not only sophisticated scholars fail to see the problem which established religions try to solve. The devoted adherents of the various forms of religion are also blind to it because they assume that the system of belief, feeling and action to which they are committed is the final solution. Consequently there is for them no problem to be solved. It already is solved. The only problem is to win popular acceptance for the faith professed by them.

When one accepts a ready-made answer without struggling with the question, he never understands the full significance of the answer, no matter how perfectly he repeats the doctrines and performs the ceremonies. He who gets the answers in the back of the book instead of working on the problem until he finds the answer for himself, will never understand the issues in scope and depth. Education must assume responsibility for the conduct of religious living not by teaching the doctrines and ceremonies nor imparting the faith but by exposing the true character and vital significance of the basic problem which the current form of faith tries to solve.

There is less popular understanding of the problem which religion tries to solve than is the case with economics, politics, government, literature and art, with the possible exception of art. There are several reasons for this. For one thing, religion for centuries has been propagated not as a question to be answered but as the final answer to a question scarcely asked. The great founders of the world religions struggled with the problem. For them religion was the question asked and they sought an answer. But for centuries the question in its tragic depth and awful issues has been concealed by popular answers accepted by individuals before they ask the question.

Another cause of blindness to the problem in the conduct of religious living is that religion has been excluded from the kind of critical examination which education gives to other major concerns of human life. Even when religion is put into education, it is done under the supervision of the church. This is like putting economics into education under the supervision and control of the big corporations. In such case the school becomes another agent for transmitting the established system of belief and practice, whether it be in economics or religion. This prevents education from assuming the responsibility which it should assume, namely, to understand the question before one accepts the answer. This does not mean that the student must repudiate the system of belief and practice prevailing in his society, whether it be in business and industry or in religion. It does mean that when he accepts the established forms he will do so with understanding of their proper function and thus will be able to participate in them not blindly but intelligently.

The churches, like the big corporations, are chiefly concerned to perpetuate and win recruits to the system of belief and practice by which they operate. This is not a condemnation of them. This is what they should do in contrast to the educational institutions. This work of church and corporation becomes pernicious only when the school fails to do its part. Worst of all it becomes pernicious when the school is subordinated to the service of the church in study of religion and to the corporation in study of economics and to the dominant political party in the study of government and to the interests controlling television and radio in the study of art.

The basic question which religion tries to answer has been repeatedly stated in previous chapters. It needs to be brought again to mind in the present context. It is this: How discover and induce men to commit themselves to what saves man as he cannot save himself, to deliver him from his self-destructive propensities and bring him to the best that human life can ever attain, provided that required conditions are met.

Salvation here refers not merely to the individual because the individual cannot be separated from society. It refers not merely to society because society cannot be separated from history. It refers to the individual in society and society in history. The salvation sought is the salvation of man, psychologically, socially, historically. It is the salvation of human life in its total movement of history, society and individual existence. It includes all that existentialism can say about the individual but this is totally misunderstood if not seen in the context of society and history. One of the tragic misunderstandings of the religious problem is due in no small part to the teaching of the great world religions. It is the notion that the individual can be saved without regard to society and history by delivering him from hell and taking him to heaven, or delivering him from endless rebirths and bringing him to Nirvana. Other religions have other interpretations of salvation just as falsely individualized.

Certainly there is no such thing as society and history apart from individuals. The individual is all-important. He only can be saved but he cannot be separated from society and history. His destiny is wrapped up in the course of society and history. There is no religion except the religion of the individual. But that does not mean that religion is a private matter. It is profoundly social and historical even as the mind and personality of the individual, down to his most hidden and intimate impulses, are what they are in part because of the society and history in which he participates. Biological heredity makes its contribution also. But it is ridiculous to try to divide the characteristics of the individual into separate compartments, one compartment due to heredity and the other to society and history. Every characteristic of the individual is shaped both by heredity and by society and history. His automatic reflexes would never occur if society had not nourished him in infancy.

Two ways of "putting religion into education" have been widely advocated in recent years. Both of them are here rejected because contrary to the interest of religion and contrary to the requirements of education. One of these is the proposal that the school limit itself to teaching *about* religion. According to this suggestion the student should be instructed concerning the part religion has played in our culture and in human culture generally. He should become acquainted with the various systems of belief, ritual and action found in the sects and faiths of mankind. If this merely means that when religion appears in a course in history it should be taught as history, of course it should be recognized for what it is. Or if it means that when religion appears in the study of anthropology or in any of the social or psychological disciplines the student should study it in the form in which it there appears, then of course that should be done. But if this means that the teacher in such cases should put in a plea for religion to protect its reputation in face of the great evils it has done, the procedure becomes pernicious and deceptive.

In any case, whether the school teaches *about* religion by recognizing the part it has played in human life as this part appears in the teaching of other subjects, or whether special courses are set up to teach about it by instructing the student concerning the facts of its existence, in neither case has the responsibility of education for the conduct of religious living been met. Teaching about religion in this way might very well be introduced as incidental and instrumental to the study of the problem which religion tries to solve. But to limit education to teaching about religion in this way would be as mistaken as it would be to limit education in economics to teaching about economic practices without any study of economic theory concerning the best way to solve the economic problem.

The second proposal here rejected for putting religion into education can best be examined by considering a specific example. One member of the Board of Education of the city of St. Louis in the autumn of 1959 suggested that the school assembly be opened every morning with a prayer. The prayer was so worded that it would not discriminate among Protestantism, Catholicism, and Judaism. It was claimed that it had been "approved for use in schools by the three major religions and by the New York State Board of Regents." The prayer was: "Almighty God, we acknowledge our dependence on Thee, and we beg Thy Blessings upon us, our parents, our teachers and our country."

Such a prayer, or any other religious ceremony intended to induce the religious attitude, would not be in the interest of religion. This can be demonstrated by an examination of the situation. Worship, or religious commitment of any kind, is not a matter of uttering certain words. To induce the attitude of worship it is necessary to have conditions favorable for it. Some adults who have practiced worship all their lives may have their attitude so deeply established that they can worship anywhere under any conditions. But this is not true of children who are only beginning to worship; and it is not true of most adults. One of the conditions which must be present to induce the worshipful response to the symbols of worship is a group of people responding to the symbols in much the same way with much the same understanding of their significance. By understanding their significance is not meant merely an intellectual formula applied to them. "Understanding the significance" here means the cultivated ability to respond to the religious symbols with the kind of religious response called worship. This kind of response requires favorable conditions. Otherwise the presentation of the symbols will not induce worship but will arouse other responses having nothing to do with worship. When this occurs, the children are being taught not to worship when the religious symbols are presented. Having in this way been taught in school not to worship in the presence of the religious ceremony, they will continue not to worship when the ceremony is practiced in home and church. Thus in the interest of religion itself, religion should not be put into the school in the form of religious ceremony, testimony and exhortation.

In the home and church and in religious groups voluntarily formed by students and others, on the campus or off, the fellowship of worship can be provided. It is not provided in the school where the great majority, namely, the students themselves, have at best only begun to learn to practice a form of religion and many have not even begun. Some will have been taught to reject, as false and unworthy, any of the major forms of religion in our culture. Thus the attempt to introduce worship and other forms of religious practice into the public school will produce consequences the opposite of which is intended.

Not only does the practice of religious ceremony and all attempts to impart the faith defeat the purpose of religion when undertaken by the public school, it also defeats the purpose of education. This follows from what has already been said about the purpose of education, namely, to enable the student to understand the problem which underlies religious practice. Students in the elementary grades are not yet sufficiently mature to understand these basic problems. Study of the religious problem should not be attempted until the student has reached college and university. Already this kind of study is a part of many colleges and universities, although it has not been developed to the point required. It has not yet become an established policy in higher education, as it must become if our civilization is to endure. Teachers and materials have not yet been developed in a way fit to deal with the problem in adequate manner. Yet it has become an urgent necessity that the conduct of religion be more intelligent, more wise and more profound than occurs in our society. This better conduct of religion cannot be achieved without the help of education after the manner here proposed.

Studying the problem which religion tries to solve in institutions of higher learning will not bring on a religious revival. But it will prepare the way for future prophets to bring forth a powerful and sustaining and creative faith. The way must be prepared by an intelligent understanding of the question before prophets can arise to proclaim the answer.

After colleges and universities have developed teachers, methods and materials for this way of studying religion, and have done it for a generation, it should be extended down to the High School, because the High School is most in need of this kind of teaching. But we should first learn how to teach the subject of religion in this way before we expose the High School to it.

If this kind of education is not established as a policy in college and university, and later in the High School, religion will continue to be transmitted as an established system but without adequate understanding of the question which the system must answer to avoid disaster. If this understanding is not attained by way of education, the established systems of religion will be changed in whatever way is required to keep them going and to compete with rival systems. But this is not the kind of change which must occur to carry the human race through the life and death struggle in which it is now engaged. The human race has always been engaged in a life and death struggle, whether or not the participants knew it. Always some solution of the religious problem was necessary to carry them into the ways of life and from the ways of death. But power, complexity and change were never so great as now. For this reason the established forms of religion must be revised to deal with the basic religious question in a way suited to the conditions of our time. This cannot be done without understanding of the problem.

A mistaken way in which institutions of higher learning have often attempted to deal with this religious problem should be avoided. They have tried to treat it as a problem in metaphysics or ontology. Doubtless ontological questions are relevant, but the religious problem is much more than an ontological problem and to treat it primarily in terms of an ontology is to leave the distinctively religious part of it untouched.

To show how the religious issues are missed when the religious question is thought to find its answer in ontology, an example is needed. The work of Paul Weiss in his *Modes of Being* serves very well to demonstrate the point. This work is chosen not because it alone fails to deal adequately with the religious problem by way of an ontology. Any work attempting to do so will illustrate the failure of this procedure. The work of Weiss is chosen not only because it is one of the most recent attempts but also because it is one of the most competent and is carried out with unusual mastery of all the resources of present-day philosophy. Consequently, if such an attempt fails, it is evidence that all other attempts will also fail when the ontological approach to the religious problem is adopted.

We have already seen how Paul Tillich's ontological approach fails. When faith comes asking for bread Tillich's ontology can only offer the stone of non-cognitive symbols, providing no descriptive knowledge of the power of being, which according to this ontology, is the source of man's salvation. The ontological approach of Charles Hartshorne and Alfred North Whitehead might also be examined to show the sterility of what they offer when faith comes asking. This does not mean that the work of these men is worthless.

Many profound and valuable insights can be gained from them. But they do not provide the kind of guidance which faith must have in committing itself to what actually operates in human life to save, transform, guide and bring to the best that human life can ever attain. To find this divine presence in human life an empirical approach must be followed, even though an ontology stands in the background.

Professor Weiss analyzes human experience to find the basic categories without which no human experience whatsoever can occur. He finds four and calls them modes of being. One mode he calls existence. It is a continuous ongoing without purpose or form except as it is ordered by other modes of being. Actualities arise within it; but it also destroys them. It might be called energy, although I do not believe Weiss uses that term in this context.

The second mode of being is actuality. Actualities are human beings, trees, stones, houses, every organized form of existence. The third mode is ideality. Ideality is possibility, prescriptive for conduct in the form of moral ideals; prescriptive for thinking in the form of logical principles; prescriptive for art and aesthetic experience.

Finally is the mode of being called God. It is the unifying agency. It provides whatever unity is found in all other modes and is what unites all the modes to one another.

Each mode has a measure of independence and self-sufficiency in itself. Yet they are also dependent upon one another, since none could be without the others. Also they overlap or infect one another; they participate in one another. None is entirely subject to the others. In that sense they resist one another so that none can unduly dominate over the others. Thus there is a degree of independence, a degree of participation in one another and a degree of opposition to one another.

The human being and other actualities exist by participating in existence. Yet the tumultuous ongoing of existency sus-

tains them only precariously and in time destroys each of
them. Human actualities participate in ideality, but only
partially and imperfectly. Thinking cannot occur without
the ideality of logic, but human thinking is only partially and
imperfectly logical. Ideality reaches beyond all human participation and has an independence and self sufficiency of its
own. Human conduct participates in moral ideality and conduct cannot be human unless it does, even when it resists
the demands of the moral ideal. Finally, every actuality is
not only a unit in itself, even when its unity is imperfect, as
it always is; but also actualities, and especially human actualities, belong to an encompassing unity, even though this
unity is tenuous at times and always subject to degrees of disintegration. This unity is the mode of being called God in
this ontology. It is one of four, no "more real," no more
sustaining, no more potent, no more necessary to our existence than are the others.

The divine mode of being has an independence and a self
sufficiency of its own to some degree, like every other mode.
In so far as this mode of being called "God" transcends its
unifying agency in our experience we cannot know what it
is. This affords Weiss the opportunity to endow these unknowable reaches of God's being with all the conventional
attributes of God found in the Christian tradition. But these
attributes are not truly descriptive of the inner being of God
because God in himself, beyond the unity he imparts to all
other modes of being, is absolutely unknowable. God is said
to be conscious, to have purpose, to love and the like. But
Weiss admits that consciousness in God is not consciousness
as it is in us, nor is the love, the purpose, the justice and all
the other personal characteristics attributed to the divine
being. This amounts to saying that these words applied to
God do not mean what they seem to mean. They refer to
what is entirely beyond our knowing and therefore have
no discoverable meaning, when "meaning" is what a word

designates or describes. They describe nothing in God. They are the same as the non-cognitive symbols used by Tillich to dress up the power of being with the semblance of the traditional idea of God. Thus Weiss answers the question asked by faith as Tillich does, with a stone of a non-cognitive symbol.

The point of this criticism is not that the fourth mode of being set forth by Weiss and given the name of God fails to conform to the traditional picture of deity even when given that appearance. It does fail to conform, but that is not the point of the criticism. The point of this criticism is that this mode of being does not operate in human life to save man as he cannot save himself, to deliver him from his self destructive propensities and lead to the greater good when required conditions are met.

The word "God" has one basic referent underlying all the diverse pictures of deity cherished in the hearts and minds of people. This basic reference designates what operates to save and transform after the manner repeatedly stated. This is the basic religious problem to be solved. The traditional and cherished pictures of deity conceal this problem and confuse the basic referent of the word so that philosophers as well as many others seem to think that if the traditional picture of deity can be retained the problem is solved. This is precisely what is meant by blindness to the religious problem, a blindness shared by philosophers along with the great mass of common people who have been taught to accept one answer to the religious question before ever they understand what the religious question truly is.

All this amounts to saying that what Weiss calls God is not God in any religious sense of the word. Weiss admits that the inquiry by which he finds the divine mode of being is not religious inquiry. Certainly it is not, when religious inquiry means to seek the answer to the question asked by faith. He does not claim that what he calls God actually operates in human life to transform man from the evil to the good.

While the mode of being called God in this ontology does not answer the question asked by faith, the analysis of experience into the four necessary components of all human experience seems valid, although it is not the only analysis which might be made. Furthermore, this analysis might be used to find our way to what answers the question of faith. Indeed this ontology serves faith much better than Tillich's.

If one adopts Weiss's ontology one could say that God is the being operating in the area where the four modes of being overlap. This fourfold being of existence, ideality, actuality and unifying power creates actuality out of existence; it creatively transforms actuality to actualize more of ideality when required conditions are present; it progressively integrates human actuality both internally and in relation to other actualities, again provided that required conditions are present. In short, God is the basic creativity operating by way of all four of the modes. But such a being must be found empirically and not alone by the analysis which yields the ontology, although this ontology opens the way for the kind of empirical inquiry which finds God.

While ontology is not the form of philosophy which can by itself alone answer the question asked by faith, it can make its own contribution. Even a greater contribution, and one more urgently needed, can be made by philosophical analysis. One of the greatest obstacles to understanding the religious problem in its true character is the vagueness, ambiguity and confusion of meanings carried by religious language. These meanings should be analyzed, the confusion reduced, the vagueness and ambiguity removed; and above all, the line of distinction should be drawn between the non-cognitive religious symbols used by faith in the practice of commitment, and the statements which can be true or false relative to available evidence. Philosophical analysis has developed powerful instruments in recent years and while it is liable to gross error at times in misunderstanding the problem which concerns the language under analysis, it can render invaluable service when education assumes responsibility for religious inquiry.

The kind of critical revision of systems of religious belief and practice here demanded should not be confused with many other kinds of revision. For example, it is common practice to modify religious systems only at those points and in those ways which make the system acceptable to the so-called "modern mind." Worst of all, the body of traditional doctrine may be reconstructed with the sole purpose of making it "intellectually respectable." Perhaps no greater degradation can befall the intellectual foundation of faith than to have it reconstructed primarily for respectability and not for the truth.

Another form of degradation, almost as bad, is to revise a body of doctrine with the sole concern to make it conform to some cherished tradition, whether the tradition is called the Christian tradition, or the Jewish tradition, or the Judaeo-Christian, or the Hindu or the Hottentot. This is degradation because tradition by itself alone is no evidence for the truth. Certainly the truth might be found in tradition. But the evidence of truth is not that it happens to be transmitted to me in my tradition. I should search my own tradition to find whatever truth may be there. But one must be able to distinguish within the total body of tradition what is true, so far as anything is true, and what is false. Furthermore, the evidence of truth cannot be simply that it conforms to the mental attitude acquired by me in the religious fellowship where I happen to have spent my formative years.

The religious problem here under consideration is not to achieve intellectual respectability, nor to conform to the modern way of thinking, nor to recover the substance of an ancient tradition. It is very different from all of these. It is to achieve a system of affirmations correctly specifying what does in truth have the character and power to transform man as he cannot transform himself, to save him from his self-destructive propensities and lead him to the best that human life can attain, provided that the required conditions are met.

The problem we are considering is indeed religious. But its supreme importance lies not in the fact that it bears the name of religion. Its importance is intrinsic to the nature of man and to the structure of human existence at levels fatefully determining the good and evil of our lives. What we commit ourselves to, will either destroy us or save us. What we commit ourselves to, *believing* that it saves from evil and unto the good, either does in truth do that, or else it does not. If it does not, our religious faith might lead us to the greatest evil. If it does, our commitment will lead toward the greatest good. This and nothing less than this, is involved in the problem of the intellectual foundation of faith. We must find out what is literally and descriptively true, and what is false, in beliefs directing the commitment of our lives.

This problem is more fatefully important today than ever before because of the gigantic power now under human control. When man had little power, his self destructive propensities could not do great harm. When he has enormous power, his self destructive propensities can do enormous harm. Therefore the question of truth and error in the intellectual foundation of our faith has become crucially important.

Since this problem has this supreme importance, it can no longer be excluded from consideration by the institutions of higher learning; nor by other institutions devoted to research on problems which determine the good and evil of life.

So far we have looked at the responsibility of education

for understanding the religious problem in its social context. Education also has responsibility for understanding the religious problem internal to the individual personality. It is the problem of releasing his full creative potentiality. These two problems cannot be separated since the solving of one depends upon solving the other. Yet they can be distinguished.

To understand the religious problem as a personal problem we turn for help to clinical psychology and the various kinds of psychology engaged in the work of psychotherapy. One of the most instructive theories based on extensive and intensive research is set forth by L. S. Kubie in *Neurotic Distortions and the Creative Process*. According to Kubie every human individual has vastly greater capacity for creative transformation of his own person, of his way of life and in his achievements, than is ever actualized.

The source of all this creativity, so far as it resides within the individual himself, is not the unconscious nor the conscious level of the mind. It is, rather, that level which lies between these two, called by Kubie the preconscious. The preconscious function of the mind achieves automatic and subtle recordings of multiple perceptions, hidden from consciousness and beyond the capacity of the conscious function. This can be demonstrated. A person is put in a room for a few minutes and then taken to another room and asked what he perceived in the first room. He may report twenty or thirty items. When put under hypnosis he can report two hundred things perceived. The preconscious has this capacity for effortless, automatic recording of multiple perceptions; also effortless and automatic recall of all of them; also the connecting of them into all manner of linkages to form new patterns. This is creativity.

But this potential creativity is blocked and cannot reach the conscious mind because of two other characteristics of the human being. One of these is the unconscious which underlies the preconscious. Of course when we say that it underlies, as though the mind had three stories, the unconscious, the preconscious and the conscious, we are using a figure of speech. But the mind does function in these three different ways and that is the point to understand.

The unconscious resists creative transformation in the organization of the personality, in the way of life and in all achievement. It blocks the emergence of new insights. It does this because of fears and hates and all manner of anxieties which cannot reach consciousness but which exercise coercive control over the functioning of the conscious and preconscious. This control is limited, and some have much more freedom than others. Freedom here does not mean exemption from causal sequence; it does mean some exemption from the obstruction imposed upon the creativity of the preconscious by hidden fears operating unconsciously.

A simple illustration will show how unconscious fears and hates and other anxieties obstruct the potential creativity of the preconscious. An individual identifies himself with some accomplishment or way of life or viewpoint or other characteristic. He comes to feel that his honor, his reputation, his virtue, his worth, his safety, his rank in the eyes of others, all or some of these depend upon holding fast against all change to some particular feature. This kind of resistance to creativity can assume many diverse forms. In all cases it is a coercion arising out of some fear, hate or other anxiety beyond the reach of conscious control.

The other restraint upon creativity is imposed by the practical necessities of consciousness. To follow the logical implications of a statement the course is pre-determined and all irrelevant deviations must be excluded. The same is true of a course of action to reach a predetermined goal or to gather evidence to test a theory. The same is true of communication when a definite structure of thought, established from the beginning, is to be presented. Only when the conscious mind is relaxed and open to the non-selected paths of free association can the creative potentialities of the preconsciousness reach the level of conscious thought, feeling and action.

All the constraints imposed upon the creativity of the preconscious come from social relations; and these in turn are shaped by the consequences of the past which is history. Thus society in the form of intimate interpersonal relations as well as all the customs and institutions and the course of history, all this enters into the creativity of the individual, either to feed and sustain it or restrict and block it. The creativity of the preconscious is nurtured or stunted by social interchange; and social interchange is more or less creative, depending on consequences derived from the past in the form of language and in the form of institutions and customs. Thus the creativity of the preconscious within the individual cannot be separated from society and history, nor can the creativity provided by society and history be separated from the functioning of the individual preconscious.

The responsibility of education is to foster the creativity of the individual. We need to know much more than we now do about the human mind, and especially about the functioning of the preconscious in relation to the unconscious and the conscious functions, before education can be shaped to do what it must do if the problems of our civilization are to be treated constructively. We already know more than we are putting into practice and we are on the way to knowing much more. As stated in the preceding chapter, billions of dollars should be put into research to discover the conditions required to release as fully as possible the creativity operating in human life. This is both a social and psychological problem and all the sciences can make important contributions. Not until all the sciences become dedicated to the religious problem along with education, can the full measure of creativity potentially resident in human life become operative as it must if man is to be saved from self destruction or degradation as his power increases and as all men come to live together in one society.[11]

CHAPTER EIGHT

FREEDOM ANSWERS

In a democracy the government should control the people and the people should control the government. This dual control is possible when the government and the people both serve a higher loyalty bringing government and people under a unifying purpose. This unifying purpose must overarch and comprehend the diverse private interests of individuals and local groups and institutions. It must not only unify; it must also stimulate each individual, to bring his total individuality into action, so far as the conditions of human existence permit. When government and people are thus united under an allegiance transcending both the private interests of those who administer the government and the private interests of those who are governed, each can strive to keep the other faithful to this ruling commitment. The people can then check and correct the government, not merely to make it serve the special private interests of the governed but rather to keep it faithful to what creates and sustains a social order in which private interests can flourish.

This theory of democracy contradicts the theory which prevailed during the nineteenth century. After the American and French revolutions, the dominant theory of democracy proclaimed that the government is the servant of the people. This was interpreted to mean that the government should serve the private interests of the governed so long as these did not run counter to one another. It was generally believed that government should be reduced to the minimum required to maintain social order, protect from the foreign foe and enforce the rules of competition or whatever other rules might be required to keep private interests from seriously obstructing one another.

This theory of nineteenth century democracy seems still to rule the minds of men or, if not their minds, at least their practice. It is true that government in the United States and other Western democracies has expanded enormously but this expansion has been driven by the necessities of action; it has not been approved by the prevailing theory. Every extension in the control of government over private interests has been resisted and has been accepted only because there seemed to be no other way to meet certain imperative needs. The chief compulsions driving the people of the democracies to accept "creeping socialism" as it has been called, have been war, disastrous economic depression and fear of its recurrence and, above all, bitter hate and fear of the spread of communism.

Creeping socialism, if one wishes to give it that name, is the consequence of the nineteenth century theory of democracy, paradoxical as that may sound. When the theory of democracy declares that the function of government is to serve private interests so long as they do not conflict, no principle can specify the form and direction of the expanding powers of government save only the demand of private interests. Consequently, when these interests are endangered by conflict among themselves, or by economic depression, or by a foreign enemy, or when the people are aroused to fear and hate communism without and subversion within, the power of government is expanded to meet each emergency. But its expansion is not guided and controlled by any principle. It is guided only by the demands of private interests. In this way government controlled by private interests becomes "creeping socialism." Also when control of government is extended to meet emergencies and without other guiding principle, the call for this extension is likely to assume the form of popular hysteria.

Democracy cannot be saved if it continues on this basis. Government controlled by hysteria of the people is dangerous. Indeed according to Walter Lippmann the decline of democracy the world around has been catastrophic, since the early years of this century.[12] No one is better informed and wisely observant of the current of world affairs than is Lippmann. His story of what has been happening and his diagnosis of the sickness of democracy is here accepted, although his suggestion of cure by reinstating natural law as the supreme principle regulating both government and private interests is not accepted. It is not accepted unless "natural law" is given a very special interpretation. This interpretation I do not find in Lippmann's account of it.

Lands proclaiming freedom as their prized possession still have wealth, technology and private initiative beyond other people. But their domain is shrinking. The unquestioned world-leadership they had in 1900 is slipping from them. Since the first world war millions have repudiated the ways of freedom. Today the people of the United States are afraid of traitors and enemies of freedom in their own homeland. They fear that democracy may be betrayed by fellow Americans as well as by enemies in other lands. The oaths of loyalty demanded of teachers and students are evidence of this fear and distrust. Freedom has been retreating before the advance of the totalitarian powers, even reaching into the heartland of this free country as shown by this fear that American citizens may be subversive.

All this is a reversal of the state of affairs in 1900. Beginning with the end of the eighteenth century democracy advanced in triumph for a hundred years. One country after another adopted the slogans of freedom and the forms of democratic control. At the beginning of the twentieth century all the world looked to the democratic powers for leadership and for instruction to learn the ways of confidence, power, private initiative and respect for the individual. Never was democracy so highly honored and its power throughout the world so great. Most leaders, certainly those in Europe and America, seemed confident that the world would adopt the economy, the political forms and the aims of education developed in the West. It was generally believed that humanity at last had found the way of life for man to follow toward his highest attainment.

The contrast between 1905 and 1960 is extreme. The triumphant march and the confident outlook have been reversed. Weakness and decay have set in. Fear and uncertainty about the security of democracy even in its own homeland are eating into the minds of the devotees of freedom. The material resources and all the instruments and skills of mastery are with us still. No other culture and no other people can compare with the West in this respect, although the communist countries are gaining rapidly. No people ever had such resources in trained minds and material goods as we. But we seem unable to use them effectively against opposing powers. The hand has lost its cunning. The mind to direct the hand no longer has the vision and the insight. This is Lippmann's diagnosis of our condition.

What is the cause of this decline? Following Walter Lippmann and others who have been observing and analyzing this development for half a century, the cause can be summarized very briefly although full understanding leads into great complexities.

Put into most abbreviated form the cause of this decline might be stated thus: The democratic peoples have come to interpret freedom in terms of private, local, competing and transitory interests. They view democracy as a utility to serve these interests and to raise the standard of living. They do not recognize as commanding their ultimate allegiance a common good underlying these private interests and sustaining them. They do not recognize the prior claim upon their devotion of that development continuous through history which creates freedom in social relations and in the mind of man. Having no such ultimate commitment the democratic peoples identify freedom with social control exercised by the changing desires, hates and fears which happen at any time to possess the mind of individuals and the voting majority. Under such conditions the leaders of democratic society cannot command great sacrifice of the people except by stirring up hate and fear to a pitch approaching hysteria. During the latter part of 1959 there was opportunity to reduce the bitter antagonism between the communist countries and the Western democracies. But many political leaders do not want to reduce the tension and the danger of the cold war because its relaxation will reduce the hate and fear required to whip up the will of the great majority to the point where they will pay the exorbitant taxes and make the other sacrifices demanded by government to meet emergencies. The slogan proclaims that we must not let down our guard, we must not relax. We must not anticipate peace nor practice good will lest our vigilance decline.

As Lippmann says, this is an ugly fact about the present political situation. It is a dangerous condition inimical to the survival of democracy. When political action must be supported by hate and fear it cannot be wise, it cannot negotiate skillfully, it cannot compromise. It must insist on "moral principle" because "moral principle" gives the appearance of righteousness to hate and fear. When these passions possess a people they must be clothed in the garments of righteousness. Otherwise the country cannot call itself Christian and on that account morally superior to countries where the Christian faith is repudiated. A people inheriting the Christian tradition must be godly and righteous in their own eyes when opposed to a godless regime.

All this has weakened the power of the democracies when dealing with problems requiring high intelligence combined with sacrifice of private interests to serve a public good continuous through history. Minds obsessed with fear and hate or with local interests and the immediate future are in no position to understand what needs to be done to protect and promote the historic continuity of what underlies and sustains freedom. On the other hand, men in positions of responsibility with access to information and counsel enabling them to understand what needs to be done cannot act in the way to sustain the historic continuity of the free society which they serve. They cannot because they must first of all win the approval of minds with no understanding nor compelling responsibility for the underlying and vital needs of freedom. Nations, cultures and ways of life survive or perish by developments spanning many generations; and if these developments are ignored, no way of life can survive for long, especially in a civilization so dynamic as ours.

This is the predicament of the democracies. It is the cause of their weakness and decay according to Lippmann and other analysts. For this reason the democracies are in retreat before the totalitarian powers and cannot act with the decision, skill and wisdom to hold their own against the rising tide of tyranny. The prestige, power, leadership and confidence once possessed by them have been draining away for half a century.

Popular blindness to the common good and public interest is increased in our time by the interpretation given to the conflict with communism and the totalitarian powers. Our enemies glorify a common good which submerges the needs and interests of the individual. Therefore, so it is said, we must magnify the unique and diverse demands of individuals, the competing and transitory goals of endeavor which happen to be most popular, the local and private interests of individuals and organized groups. But this is a false alternative. There is a common good which underlies the aggregate of private interests and sustains the free society. This is what the government should serve and protect above all else.

This common good is the creative interchange described throughout previous chapters. This good is common not only to one nation and one people, although it is certainly that. But it is also the good common to all mankind and to all the ages of human history. It is what sustains and promotes freedom. When the government acts to provide and protect conditions most favorable for this kind of appreciative understanding between diverse groups and interests, the aggregate of private interests will flourish most freely and attain most abundantly what they seek. But freedom cannot be defended if political action is guided by whatever private interests happen to be organized in such a way that they can bring pressure and other influence to bear upon men in high office.

The good common to all is not the state; neither is it the chaotic aggregate of private interests; neither is it economic production pouring out consumer goods in such abundance that people have little time for anything else than to consume all the gadgets produced under high pressure of salesmanship, advertising, installment buying and built-in obsolescence. The common good is not anything which submerges the individual. The common good is what releases and develops all the constructive potentialities of the individual. The common or public good is the creativity which does this for everyone when required conditions are present. A government dedicated to freedom must provide these conditions so far as political action can provide them. No government can do this if it is guided by whatever the majority of the people happen to desire. It must be guided by intelligent understanding of what the conditions may be for creative interchange. As society changes, these required conditions change; but the essential character of the public and common good does not change. Always the common good is the free and full development of the individual in such relation to other individuals that their interchange releases each from the unconscious and conscious fears and hates distorting and suppressing their creative potentialities.

The government cannot itself provide this common good but it can provide many of the conditions under which this kind of interchange will prevail over counter processes throughout the society over which it has jurisdiction. Therefore to identify freedom with the desires of a voting public is to betray the cause of freedom when the people have not been informed concerning the conditions of freedom and when their minds are diverted by advertising, salesmanship and preoccupation with paying off debts incurred through buying on credit what they do not need. Freedom cannot be sustained by the will of the people unless their will is directed to conserving and improving the necessary conditions of freedom. As explained in a previous chapter, the people can have this will to freedom only if they have access to the kind of education and religious commitment whereby such a will is generated.

If the necessary conditions of a free society are known, and if the allegiance of the people is given to what in truth creates and sustains freedom, the people will accept the authority of the government when it acts to uphold the basic conditions of freedom. Such knowledge and such allegiance enable the people to control the government and the government to control the people in a way to sustain freedom with all the resources of a mighty civilization. But without such knowledge and without such allegiance cultivated and widely disseminated, the greater the power of the civilization the more swiftly and disastrously will it destroy its own freedom.

The problem is to find what calls for the ultimate allegiance of those who fight for freedom; what calls for the sacrifice of private interests in service of the common good and public interest; what the government should protect and promote, not by obeying the demands of mass opinion and special interests within the body politic, but by commanding these all in concerted action to serve what is deeper and greater and more precious than these demands.

Local groups and private interests must be represented in the government; they must be considered and served. But to serve them and follow the guidance of the uninformed man on the street in a way to destroy the sources of freedom is to serve the people treacherously even when the treachery is unintended.

The problem is to serve a good which is common to all because it is of such character that, if given priority over private interests in the conduct of government, it will satisfy the needs of each unique individual more abundantly than is possible when government is controlled by conflicting, transitory and local interests. Stating the same thing in reverse order, conflicting, transitory and local interests will be served more richly by the government if it gives primary concern not directly to these interests but to what underlies them and is common to them all.

The executive branch of government in our society as now ordered does not have the independence and power of command which any government must have to use the wisdom and control the resources available to it. Only the executive is in a position to understand and act intelligently on many matters vital to the common good and sometimes necessary to the survival of the democratic way of life. Over against the executive are the representatives of the people. They serve the interests expressed and promoted by organized groups and these are private and local. It is the duty of the representatives to serve these interests but on that very account they cannot have the perspective and responsibility fitting them to act wisely and independently of local interests in service of what underlies and comprehends these diverse and transitory demands.

The people who benefit from democratic government, says Lippmann, no longer understand and accept the principles which sustain democracy. Furthermore, they are anxious and lonely because they have no communion with one another in sharing common convictions concerning what commands the ultimate allegiance of men and what should be the direction of human striving. Therefore, they have no shared allegiance which can unite them in defending and upholding democracy. Ultimate allegiance is left to the interpretations of private judgment so that no ruling devotion can unite the adherents of democracy. This is a fatal weakness, says Lippmann. Under such conditions the democracies cannot hold their own against social systems upheld by a dedicated elite who are united by shared convictions concerning what should be the goal of all human living and who are committed to it above all private interests, regardless of the error and evil of these convictions.

Few are better informed than Lippmann concerning what is actually going on in the world; few are more deeply concerned for freedom and few have shown more profound insight into social issues in books and other public statements running through many years of comment with world-wide observation and personal contact with men in positions of highest responsibility. If anyone has had opportunity to find out what is wrong with us, it is Lippmann. That does not make him infallible. He may be mistaken but it is folly to thrust his ideas aside without serious consideration.

The key thought in his treatment of the problem of power in a free society is stated in the following quotation.

The power of the executive has become enfeebled, often to the verge of impotence, by the pressures of the representative assembly and of mass opinions. This derangement of the governing power has forced the democratic states to commit disastrous and, it could be, fatal mistakes. It has also transformed the assemblies in most, perhaps not in all, democratic states from the defenders of local and personal rights into boss-ridden oligarchies, threatening the security, the solvency, and the liberties of the state.[13]

What is the cause of this derangement of the two functions, one to govern, the other to represent? What has given such dominance to the function of representing so that the other function, namely, governing, has become enfeebled to the verge of impotence? Lippmann replies to this question. He says it is caused first of all by the enormous increase in taxes and other sacrifices which the government had to demand of the people since the first world war. Since the representatives of the people must grant such demands and the people must be persuaded to approve, the government was placed in the predicament of submitting the course of public action to the judgment of the people. This inability of the government to make major decisions without popular approval results in subordinating the informed and responsible judgment of the government to the uninformed, slogan-ridden, diverse and competing interests of the multitude. These interests in turn find most effective expression in organized groups formed to promote special interests.

A further cause of weakness in democratic government should be noted. Men in high position are elected by the people and must win votes and retain popular favor by appealing to popular interests. But the minds of the people, as previously stated, are given over to the problems of using and buying the goods produced by our economic system and this system, in turn, must sell these goods in ever increasing quantity to avoid economic depression and extensive unemployment. People thus preoccupied cannot think seriously and persistently about the problems determining the future course of history and the fate of democracy. Consequently, they elect to high office individuals who promise to help them to produce, sell and consume more goods. Hence leaders are not elected who discuss basic problems outside of the interest of this voting majority. Thus men most devoted to conserving the historic continuity of freedom through the tumultuous social changes of our time, and most competent to deal with such problems, are least fitted to win high office by popular vote. This gives political advantage to leaders serving special interests and voicing the hates and fears of the passing day in disregard of the fateful issues shaping the major currents of human life.

As all men are drawn into a single society and into a total movement of human existence, and as this movement becomes more massive, operating with instruments of power gigantic in scope of control, the responsibilities of government extend more deeply into the complexities of social existence and involve possibilities reaching farther into the future. Under such conditions it is folly to think that democracy can be sustained without continuous education of the people, so continuous, indeed, that education must be put on a parity with economic production as the way in which people earn their living, not only as teachers, but as students.

The democracies have ample resources for resisting and turning back the massive repudiation of freedom which seems to be sweeping the world. But they cannot use these resources in the struggle against the foes of freedom until the government gains sufficient popular support to exercise the knowledge and wisdom available to it.

This problem to be solved by the democracies might be viewed as that of avoiding the two horns of a dilemma. One horn is to avoid that weakening of the government which results when executive decisions are in bondage to the local, conflicting and uninformed interests of the people. The other horn is to avoid that ignoring of these interests of the people which result when executive decisions are not in bondage to the judgments of the people.

Private interests are precious because they express the needs of localities, groups and individuals which are truly different from one another. These must be expressed and satisfied so far as possible. But these diverse and changing demands must not be allowed to obstruct the action required to defend and strengthen what sustains them. Zeal for the golden eggs must not kill the goose that lays them. The struggle of each unique individual, each unique locality, each unique business organization or other organized group to get the special kind of golden egg it needs or wants will kill the goose, unless some agency cares for the goose. The unsolved problem of the democracies is to untie the hands of government at the top level so that they can sustain the overall social order which makes it possible for local and private interests to flourish. Otherwise the local and private interests will kill the social system which sustains them. This is the problem of democracy in our time, as seen by Lippmann.

Lippmann's diagnosis of our malady seems altogether convincing. His proposal for its cure does not. As said before, the cure he proposes is to restore reverence for natural law. He admits that "natural law" has many meanings. If natural law can be interpreted to mean the conditions required for the operation of that kind of interchange which creates the human mind and the human way of life and all the highest good of human life, then the suggestion takes on plausibility. But these conditions cannot be identified with any final ideal order. These conditions change as the human mind develops, as society becomes more complex and technology changes our way of life. Also these required conditions must be discovered and demonstrated by observation of the way creative interchange operates under different conditions. For these reasons it would be misleading to call the conditions necessary for the existence of a free society by the name of natural law.

Lippmann says our salvation must be accomplished by a philosophy; but no philosophy can accomplish what is needed unless "philosophy" is understood to include a commitment taking priority over local and private interests and over all else in human life. Such a commitment is more than philosophy; it is religion. It requires rituals, ceremonies and assemblies practiced to cultivate and deepen this commitment and extend it to all people who will accept it. Lippmann seems to recognize this, but uses the word "philosophy" and not "religion" for another reason. Religion is commonly identified with beliefs not subject to the tests of reason. Lippmann is right in thinking that no allegiance can enable us to deal effectively with the problems of our time unless its rightful priority over other interests can be rationally demonstrated. No presentation of the ultimate good in form of myth and symbol subject to devious and changing interpretations can guide us into the ways of righteous freedom unless these myths and symbols are conjoined with definite propositions subject to testing by empirical and rational methods.

Certainly myths and symbols will be used and should be used to express and guide the actual content of living because actual living is always more than the structures entering into it. These structures, and only they, can be known and demonstrated by rational methods. The thronging content of life must be lived and for this living song and story, myth and legend, great art and profound symbol are required. While all this is true, it is equally imperative that we have statements correctly specifying the structure distinguishing this way of life. Furthermore, these statements must be confirmed by rational and empirical methods. As said before, this does not deny the need for non-cognitive symbols inspiring, sustaining and communicating the way of life having this structure. Song and praise for the flowing content, true statement for the structure, both are needed. "My cup runneth over," the psalmist says. The cup has a structure and it should be correctly described; but the running over must be expressed by the symbolism of art. These two kinds of symbols, the literal and the poetic, should not be confused nor should one be used as though it could do the work of the other.

The need to specify with description the structure containing that process which sustains freedom has led Lippmann to say that "public philosophy" and not "public religion" must be restored if freedom is to live in the world as it is now developing. He is correct in demanding that literal truth must be had. He is also correct in thinking that religion generally has lived by myth and symbol not literally true.

These symbols have been *expressive* of a way of life rather than *descriptive* of any structure pertaining to that way of life. But this only exposes the imperative from which we cannot escape if we are to be saved from the degradation of a political system without freedom. The imperative is that we develop a religion conducted *both* by the non-cognitive symbol expressing the content of life lived in the religious way and also conducted by statements specifying correctly the distinguishing structure of the divine presence which saves and transforms when men give themselves to its sovereign control.

If democracy and freedom are to be saved these are the requirements: Demonstrable truth concerning the common good underlying and sustaining the diversity of private and local interests but not identical with any part or whole of them; secondly, a form of religion leading men to trust and commit themselves to the common good, thus allowing the government to command the resources and concerted action required to sustain and serve this common good; thirdly, education for everyone whose entire work-time is not occupied with economic production and distribution, this education to be continuous and intensive study of the major problems of social existence, including the historic continuity of what sustains the society of free men. This study will be both social and religious, if rightly conducted, because the social problems will reach down to the creativity calling for religious commitment.

These three requirements—the truth, the faith and the education—must focus on what creates progressively and in wholeness the individual in community with others. All this will not insure that executives in positions of responsibility will always serve the common good. Neither will it keep the people faithful, intelligent, informed and cooperative with the government. He who anticipates perfection will be disillusioned and probably become a cynic so that his last state will be worse than the first. Nothing here said should be interpreted as promising the Kingdom of God forthwith. Fallibility and corruption will continue to play their part in human life. But life can be better or worse; and to ignore this distinction is to be as foolish as one who anticipates perfection.

The form of religion we need must be liberal religion

when "liberal" means a faith that demands the tests of reason for its affirmations. The liberal religion now prevailing does not have the maturity for undertaking the responsibility imposed upon it by the needs of our time. It is immature and irresponsible because it lacks clarity and agreement on what has the character and power to save human kind from self-destructive propensities and lead to the best that human life can ever attain. It is immature and irresponsible because it does not even undertake persistent and devoted inquiry to discover and demonstrate and communicate what does in truth have this character and power. Rather it leaves this most difficult and profound problem to the casual and uninstructed thinking of each individual.

The prevailing form of liberal religion is immature and irresponsible because it does not set up institutions so endowed and equipped that dedicated men can give their whole lives to inquiry and teaching concerning this problem of religious commitment. It is irresponsible because it assumes that the most profound problems of human existence can be adequately treated when individuals "think for themselves" without intensive, continuous and instructed study.

Liberal religion must never try to compel men to think alike nor try to induce any man to believe what does not seem to the individual to be demonstrably true. But that is only the negative part of a liberal faith and the easy part. When liberal religion stops with that it is immature and irresponsible. Liberal religion becomes positive and responsible only when it marshals all its powers to provide and equip at least some men for life-long and dedicated inquiry into the problems which concern religious faith and then endeavors to proclaim as widely and persuasively as possible what this inquiry seems demonstrably to discover.

The prevailing form of liberal religion is immature and irresponsible because it promotes a miscellany of social reforms without penetrating to that depth where personality is progressively created and the course of history is determined. Consequently it cannot have the comprehensive perspective, the history-making purpose and the driving power of a saving faith.

Last to be mentioned is the most serious defect of current religious liberalism. It is most serious because most self defeating. It is failure to recognize that freedom requires conformity at one point. People can be free only to the measure that they are committed to what creates and sustains freedom. Therefore freedom requires conformity at the point of ultimate religious commitment. Unless people hold supreme over all else what makes for freedom, they cannot be free. Unless they all agree to unite on giving first priority to what creates freedom, their freedom will drain away. Freedom means the free, full development of unique individuality. One kind of diversity is the mark of freedom—the diversity of individuality freely and fully developed and brought into action with all its resources uninhibited. But this diversity of freedom is possible only to the measure that all conform in giving first place to what makes it possible.

When liberal religion means diversity on what should be accepted as Lord and Master of life and when this diversity results in giving supreme place to many different things which do not create and sustain freedom, then liberal religion in that form is not the kind of religion which promotes freedom.

Much confusion and controversy have arisen in trying to answer the question, What is freedom of the individual? Perhaps the chief source of confusion is the mistaken notion that freedom of choice is uncaused choice. Careful examination of the implications of uncaused choice reveals that it would be the most dangerous and intolerable thing that could happen in human life. Some try to guard against the chaos and destruction that would result from uncaused choice by saying that all choice is caused except for a limited area within which choice is uncaused. But all attempts to define this area only produces more confusion and controversy. Also this limited area of uncaused choice can be as dangerous and destructive as any.

An individual is free to the measure that a cause acting on him brings the organized unity of his total self into action. No man is fully free because no man is an organized unity in complete perfection. Always there are inner conflicts below the level of consciousness. If one refuses to talk of the unconscious and insists on discussing observable behavior, it comes to the same thing. When all the subtle forms of behavior of the total organism are minutely examined, these conflicts are discovered. This inner conflict means that one part of the total self resists other parts. To the measure that one part of me resists another part of me my freedom is limited by that much.

A man's freedom is measured by the degree to which a cause brings his total self into action to determine the further consequences of the cause. On the other hand, to the measure that his own mind does not determine the consequences, he lacks freedom. For example, when a man is pushed, he may fall down. His falling down is not an act of freedom any more than a stone is free when pushed over. But when a man is pushed, he not only falls. The push also causes him to feel, think, plan, form a purpose and carry it into action. Thus the push has two kinds of effects. The one effect—falling down—is not a case of freedom. The other effect of the cause is an instance of freedom because the individual as a thinking, planning, purposing self is caused to act in a way to shape the further consequences beyond the immediate fall.

Every cause acting on an individual has these two kinds of effects. The one kind is causation without freedom; the other kind is causation with freedom. The individual is free when the sequence of cause and effect runs like this: Cause brings the total self into action; the total self in action determines the further consequences of that cause.

With this understanding of freedom it can be demonstrated that creative interchange creates and sustains freedom and increases freedom to whatever maximum it can ever attain. Creative interchange creates appreciative understanding of the unique individuality of one another. When this occurs the individuals can be their unified selves. When this does not occur, especially in infancy and childhood, the individual must act to meet the demands of the adults, or to resist those demands. In either case he builds up inner conflicts. He must be a good boy when deep within he resists being a good boy. He does not touch the hot stove because mama will slap his hand if he tries, but he still wants to touch it. He plays the part of a cute little boy to win the admiration of the adults but he has other impulses running counter to all this cuteness. Much the same occurs in the life of the adult. He plays the part of a perfect gentleman but deep within are hates and fears resisting this demand. He gives his money at the point of the gun but inwardly resists the coercion to give his money.

To the measure that each can see and feel the situation from the standpoint of the other and make this viewpoint of the other his own, so that his own original view is combined with the view of the other, the conduct of each is guided by this double vision of the situation. Each can then choose and act with his total unimpeded self because his total self is equipped with this comprehensive vision composed of the two views integrated into a total view.

When a man's vision of the situation is comprehensive and far-reaching because he has learned the views of many people and integrated them into a total view, his freedom is increased. It is increased because in this relation to others he will develop less inner conflict and will be a more completely unified self, able to bring more of his total individuality into action. Also when a man has this most comprehensive vision he can foresee alternative possibilities more extensively and accurately and thus more adequately control the consequences of any cause acting on him. Also by learning from others through acquiring their vision and other resources, he has more ability to control consequences. Finally, when people interact in this way, each can win more cooperation from others in controlling consequences. In this way freedom reaches its maximum.

All this shows that the individual develops greatest freedom in a society where creative interchange is dominant over other kinds of processes. Since this is so, people can have freedom to the measure that there is no diversity in what they accept as supremely important and to which they commit themselves in religious faith. When this ultimate commitment is the same for all, there can be maximum diversity in the form of free and full development of unique individuality and free and full expression of individuality in action.

Where this interchange prevails, individuals and groups and organizations can control one another by way of concern for one another's needs and interests and thus be liberated from the coercive and regimented control. Coercive and regimented control must be imposed to preserve the social order when mutual control is lacking.

Where this kind of interchange prevails the individual can most fully develop the constructive potentialities of his own individuality because in such a society these potentialities are recognized and valued.

When allegiance to this kind of interchange is dominant over other loyalties, the individual can identify himself with the most comprehensive purpose to be found in society and history and thus endow his life with vision of widest scope and deepest reach.

When both government and people unite in service of this kind of interchange, the people will give to their government the authority and power to decide and act to protect and promote conditions required for this creativity. They will do this even when they are not able to understand the complex issues involved provided that they know the government seeks to promote creative interchange. If religiously committed, they will do this even when great sacrifice of private interests may be demanded. Also with this commitment the people will have a guiding principle for judging who is fit for high office in terms other than the ability to pander to private interests or to win popularity by personal charm.

Such an allegiance widely prevalent will keep the government more or less under the control of the people and the people under the control of the government, since both are controlled by a ruling concern for the kind of interchange giving power and value to all.

These words are not a prediction that such a happy outcome will be achieved. Rather the foregoing statements are an attempt to point out the direction in which we must move to avoid great evils. It is an attempt to establish a standard for judging what is better and what is worse. When we know the direction of the greater good we know what to live for and what to die for, whether or not we succeed. What we need to know is not the way to sure success. Ways so proclaimed are illusions, even when the success is said to lie "beyond history," because the human mind cannot predict the future with certainty.

What we need to know is the evil to fight and the good to serve. This is so regardless of what the outcome may be in terms of success or failure. The evil to fight is a society where money, honor, promotion and prestige are given not to the fully developed individual but to some sham and pretense or some distorted fragment of the total self in action.

The evil to fight is a society where fully developed individuality is like a sore thumb, serving only to get deeply and incurably hurt, so that one must amputate "the sore thumb." In psychological language this amputation means to suppress individuality to the point where it disappears from conduct and is even lost to the consciousness of the individual himself. His own individuality disappears so completely from consciousness that he would be shocked if it rose up and stared him in the face. Who are you? he cries in pale faced fright before this ghost of what he might have been. This ghost may rise up in dreams of sleep but it will not ordinarily disturb the artificial self, polished and fitted to play the game of life according to rules excluding the fully developed individual. He plays the game with zeal and efficiency in order not to suffer the shock of encounter with the ghost of what he might have been.

Occasionally one meets a man of integrity amid all the hurts and defeats imposed by society on such a one. I remember one in particular. He was a very great man but if you ask me what I mean by calling him "great," I would find it difficult to tell you. I can tell of the occasion when intense physical pain could not keep him from doing what he felt he had to do. I can tell of the sensitivity under attack, of the treachery of friends on whom he counted, and the steadfastness with which he held to his course through it all. I can tell of the honesty with which *he admitted his failure* after he had put every ounce of strength and devotion and all the resources of his life into the undertaking. But all these are only glimpses and hints into what I mean by greatness.

The point is that he brought his whole individuality and his total self into action, combined with sensitive and profound appreciation of other individuals.

A student once asked me: Why bring your total self into action with full release of all its powers so far as possible? Why not dip and sip and float and drift? Why not cringe and run when that is the easiest way? Why not get a little kick out of this and a little tickle out of that? Why not settle down and have a good time?

I could not answer that question because he had lost the capacity to understand the answer. He who cannot find the answer to that question in his own self, can never be told because he will not understand. I say, he will not understand.

A free society will have much evil and much pain of body and mind but it will be a society where people will not have lost the capacity to understand the answer to that question.

NOTES

1. See *Neurotic Distortions and the Creative Process* by L. S. Kubie, University of Kansas Press, 1958.

2. See "Being-in-Reality" by Maurice Natanson. *Philosophy and Phenomenological Research*, Vol. XX, No. 2, December 1959, pp. 231-237.

3. *Handbook of Christian Theology*, p. 153, Living Age Books, Meridian Books Inc., N. Y., 1958.

4. *Systematic Theology*, Vol. II, p. 148.

5. *Dogmatics in Outline* by Karl Barth. Harper Torchbooks, 1959, p. 39. All quotations from Karl Barth in this chapter will be taken from this book. It summarizes his main ideas scattered through many volumes and is his latest statement.

6. *Ibid.*, p. 20.

7. *Ibid.*, pp. 57-8. Italics are Barth's.

8. Jakob Burckhardt in *Reflections on World History* quoted by Ernst Cassirer in *An Essay on Man*, p. 259.

9. Every complex society must have a social mechanism. The question is: Does the mechanism promote creative interchange and the development of each individual or does it do the opposite. The term "global mechanism" refers to a system which does the opposite.

10. See *Neurotic Distortions and the Creative Process* by L. S. Kubie.

11. What is here reported from L. S. Kubie concerning the creativity of the preconscious is not intended as a solution of the problem. Doubtless the matter is much in dispute among psychologists. The report is made only to illustrate the kind of problem involved in seeking the better to increase the creativity of the individual.

12. *Essays in the Public Philosophy* by Walter Lippmann. Little, Brown and Company. 1955.

13. *Ibid.*, pp. 54-55.

INDEX